Principled Policing

Protecting the Public with Integrity

John Alderson

WATERSIDE PRESS
WINCHESTER

Preface

We have grown accustomed to the way in which police officers act and how the function of policing is carried out. Typically, our reviews of policing are initiated by particular incidents, which call us to question specific aspects of police actions, police operations or police behaviour. In recent years examinations of policing have also been driven by the apparently more mundane agendas of 'new public management', with its emphasis on 'effectiveness and efficiency'. Whatever the source of our concerns about policing there has been a tendency to focus on the question of what the police *do*, rather than what the police *are*, to limit horizons to the study of how well the police do what they do, rather than what they are there *for*. It is to John Alderson's great credit that, both as a practicing senior police officer and as a 'police academic', he has always counselled against the narrower focus and encouraged us to ask the more fundamental questions about policing. His mission has been to develop nothing less than a 'philosophy of policing'—*Principled Policing* is the latest stage in that mission.

The search for a philosophy of policing can sometimes be dismissed as being too divorced from the realities of police work 'on the ground'. John Alderson makes a convincing case against this view. Early in this book he outlines a formula for police leadership and management, applied during his own time as a chief constable, which starts with a statement of policing *philosophy*, and moves from that foundation to *ideas*, *policies* and ultimately to *performance*. He argues that the first priority for a police leader—referred to here as 'high police'—should be to develop a fully articulated policing philosophy and a firm set of policing principles. From this level all else in the business of policing should flow. For example, the way in which police officers deal with the policing of a political demonstration can be shaped by the principles espoused by senior police command on the legitimacy of political protest itself. Taking this particular policing problem, John Alderson shows how a continuous line can be drawn from the fundamental principles held by the chief police officer, through to police tactics, right down to the standards of behaviour exhibited by front-line officers.

John Alderson's own preference is for philosophy which draws upon 'social contract' theory and is inextricably tied in with notions of justice, fairness and pursuit of the 'common good'. It is also one which places great value of the principle of *tolerance*. At one point in this book the author makes a plea for policing to aim at a state of order he describes as 'orderly disorder'. As John Alderson expresses it:

Principled Policing

Protecting the Public with Integrity

John Alderson CBE, QPM, barrister-at-law is a police writer and scholar whose work is of international repute. His books and papers have been translated into many languages (from Icelandic to Chinese) and are currently in use in police institutions worldwide.

His police career, spanning 36 years, began as a foot patrol officer in the North of England. He later held some of the highest and most influential positions in British policing, including Commandant of the National Police Staff College, Bramshill and Assistant Commissioner, New Scotland Yard: his career culminating in his appointment as chief constable of Devon and Cornwall where, as a proponent of community policing, he developed its theory and initiated its early practice.

In 1982 he was commissioned by the Council of Europe Committee for Education in Human Rights to write the European textbook for the training of European police officials, *Human Rights and the Police* (Strasbourg, 1984). His other published works include *The Police We Deserve* with P J Stead (Woolfe, 1973), *Policing Freedom* (Macdonald and Evans, 1979) and *Law and Disorder* (Hamish Hamilton, 1984).

He was visiting professor of police studies at the University of Strathclyde from 1983 to 1988, has held fellowships at Cambridge, Oxford, Exeter and Portsmouth universities, and holds doctorates (*Honoris Causa*) from the universities of Exeter (Law) and Bradford (Letters).

Principled Policing
Protecting the Public with Integrity

Published 1998 by
WATERSIDE PRESS
Domum Road
Winchester SO23 9NN
Telephone or Fax 01962 855567
INTERNET:106025.1020@compuserve.com

ISBN Paperback 1 872 870 71 6

Cataloguing-in-Publication Data A catalogue record for this book can be obtained from the British Library

Printing and binding Antony Rowe Ltd, Chippenham

Cover design John Good Holbrook Ltd, Coventry.

Policing should seek to help produce a climate in which the politics of creative disorder may have a part to play. In a sense the policing of people *en masse* requires the capacity to give gently, as a tree may bend with the wind — but to hold firm when it is vital to do so.

Those who espouse the contemporary doctrine of 'zero-tolerance' would be well advised to take heed of this message. The principle of tolerance in policing is one which accepts and respects social diversity and one which stands firm against police authoritarianism. It is also one which guides the way to more effective policing—indeed, this was exactly the case set out by the architects of the British police in the early nineteenth century. An unbending adherence to the principle of zero-tolerance is exactly the kind of bad 'philosophy' which can lead to unethical police practices on the ground and, ultimately, to the social alienation of those whose behaviour is not to be 'tolerated'.

In this encyclopedic study John Alderson takes the reader through time and space in order to demonstrate his thesis. At one point he examines the rationale behind the policing of the occupied territories during the Second World War, at another the tactics used in the policing of the picket lines in the 1984-5 miner's strike in Britain. He draws lessons from the standing of the People's Liberation Army in China as well as from the conduct of the US National Guard during the anti-Vietnam War demonstrations in the 1960s. He does not do this as a means of arriving at easy conclusions—that policing is done well here and badly there. On the contrary, he shows how in many ways the dilemmas confronting 'high police' are *universal*—it is the response to those dilemmas that differs. In this respect the author makes it clear that policing is both a *dependent* and *independent variable*. Policing cannot be understood in isolation from the political, ideological, social and cultural environment in which it operates. The policing function and the police organization are very much shaped by that environment. However, policing has its own role to play, positively and negatively, and is not simply driven by external forces. In discussing the events surrounding the Brixton disorders in Britain in the early 1980s, the author illustrates how decisions and actions of the police contributed in their own special way to the problems of social order in inner cities. Whilst the underlying causes of the Brixton disorders were undoubtedly linked to social and economic deprivation, local policing methods, reflecting a policing 'philosophy' more oriented to law-enforcement than to peace-keeping, only served to inflame events. Using this and many other examples, John Alderson demonstrates that chief officers *can* make a difference.

A central appeal of *Principled Policing* lies with its straightforward message that 'good policing' flows from sound principles. The principles that John Alderson recommends to us are bound to notions of justice, fairness, tolerance and a deep sense of community. He has been preaching these principles for many years. We have not always had the sense to listen. As we enter an era in which criminal justice policy is re-built around a concern for 'social exclusion' and a heavy commitment to social crime prevention and 'partnership', we should go back to the writings of John Alderson. He was right all along.

Professor Stephen Savage
Director, Institute of Police and Criminological Studies
University of Portsmouth

August 1998

Principled Policing
Protecting the Public with Integrity

CONTENTS

Acknowledgements

I am indebted to all those people from whose work I have been able to advance the purpose of this book. In particular I am indebted to Donald Hudson, formerly Reader in Philosophy at the University of Exeter for advice and encouragement with the basic tenets set out in *Chapter 1*, to Pastor Dr. Dieter Beese for advice on *Chapter 3* and to Edith Skingle for translations of German texts. The late General Richard Clutterbuck kindly discussed the Northern Ireland issues with me for *Chapter 5*. Roger Graef's book *Talking Blues* has been especially helpful towards *Chapter 7*, and my Chinese friendships have led to a better *Chapter 8*. To both Roger Busby for his communications skills and to Bryan Gibson, my editor, for his constructive support, I offer sincere thanks. Finally, my thanks to Elizabeth for her patience, devotion and skill in producing order out of chaos. For any errors of fact in the book the responsibility is mine.

John Alderson
July 1998

For the innocent victims of the world's unprincipled policing

Introduction

Scholarly interest in police affairs, especially in the West, increased considerably during the latter part of the twentieth century. What had been the province of a few historians and police biographers became an area of considerable interest in the burgeoning schools of sociology, with the occasional legal contribution. Literature on the police which is the product of experience has been less prolific. In *Principled Policing: Protecting the Public with Integrity* I have tried to amalgamate my practical police experience with theory.

In the study of police principles it is essential to take account of both *formal* and *informal* policing if a degree of truth about the subject is to be discovered, for the term 'police' has two meanings—and it is important to clarify their usage: on the one hand the term is used to describe the *organization* of people acting as officials in the enforcement of the edicts of those in authority; whilst on the other it is used to mean policing as in *self-policing*—through cultural, social, and other forces such as conventions, associations and institutions of what is called society, and which bring about desirable modifications of human behaviour.

Policing by 'the police' as a coercive arm of government, or the state, is therefore to be distinguished from those aspects of civil society which in themselves are conducive to a state of good order. If self-policing, and voluntary social policing were adequate, there would be no need for the police at all.

Policing by custom for mutual benefit made sense to people long before formal codes led to the introduction of officials to enforce the laws. From primeval groups based on the family, and groups of families, and later on under forms of 'parental' or 'group' authority like *pater familias* and *patria potestas*—such as existed with regard to tribes—order was maintained through habit and custom.[1] It can also be observed that the more developed and complex a society becomes, the more it depends on a multiplicity of laws and their enforcement, rather than on superstition, myth, divine providence, or on mere informal moral motivations.

There is a further important point to be borne in mind, and this concerns the juxtaposing of the *sciences* and *arts* of policing. Nowhere is this duality better illustrated than in the comparison between the science of police management and the art of police leadership. The former, is based on the efficacy of proven formulae, and the latter on intuition, flair, judgment, and adaptability when facing the unknown, untried or unexpected.

11

In a colourful passage in the introduction to his famous treatise *On War*,[2] the nineteenth century Prussian soldier and scholar, Carl von Clausewitz explained:

> Nowhere has the philosophical argument been evaded, but where it runs into too thin a spread the author has preferred to cut it short, and fall back upon the results of experience; for in the same way as many plants only bear fruit when they do not shoot too high, so in the practical arts the theoretical leaves and flowers must not be made to sprout too far, but kept near to experience which is their proper soil.

Although I approve of Clausewitz's comments on the need to extend theory with practice, the dogma which flowed from his writing ought prudently to be avoided, since excessive emphasis on purely military factors in Prussian war studies is alleged to have led to costly attrition in the conduct of the First World War. The same may be said of excessive emphasis on police efficiency in the Prussian polizeistaat, which was in some ways the precursor of the Nazi totalitarian police state. The 'proper soil' of policing then is also that of experience, modified, tempered and oriented by use of the wisdom and riches of scholarship, of which the beneficences are to be found in diverse theories.

Throughout *Principled Policing* I have tried to seek out and employ philosophical and other products of 'great and good minds' to illuminate knowledge acquired from my practice and experience. I have also tried to illustrate with examples from history (including recent history) that unprincipled policing, functioning without a moral basis, poses a real threat to liberal democracy. The examples I have selected are from France, Germany, America, Northern Ireland, China and also here in England. I could have replicated these many times over from around the world, where all too often policing has become detached from morality and sometimes from any semblance of humanity. I hope my analysis will emphasise the need for vigilance at a time when the subject of Human Rights is increasingly under scrutiny.

Ultimately, the study of police is an eclectic one, in which the abstract and the concrete both have their place. I also hope that my commentaries will provide a modest contribution to a vigorous pursuit of knowledge and understanding of policing for those whose lives and interests are touched by it.

John Alderson July 1998

Endnotes

1 Maine, Sir Henry, *Ancient Law*, Dent: London, 1917
2. Clausewitz, C von, *On War*, Penguin: London, 1968.

Part I

Theories and Principles

CHAPTER 1

Police, Government and Society: A Search for Principles

> This account begins a search for principles. It is about some fundamental
> characteristics of societies, and of their governance. It is about what I call,
> 'Principled Policing'.

The cruder ideas for the application of force to complicated social, cultural, and political situations, can at times only make matters worse. Take for example the Brixton, London disorders of 10 to 12 April 1981, when three days of rioting followed a heavy handed police operation of harassment.[1] And yet principled policing has to garner a residual strength with which to protect and preserve a fundamentally decent social order. After many years as a police official, and latterly an academic, I believe that some areas of this subject are grey ones requiring the searchlight of scrutiny and exposition.

We would all wish to live in societies which are so self-policing that coercive policing by the state would not be necessary, but this Utopia has to remain a dream. If we are to have policing arrangements they must be of the best; which does not mean the most economically expensive. The best policing has to begin with its principles.

In some countries a citizen might find fundamentals of policing in written constitutions, in others he may not. Some, as in the United Kingdom, may have to begin their search for principles in the ordinary law of the land. Principled policing should be of such a nature that it applies to all people in all societies, since it concerns reconciliation of the maintenance of order with the protection of freedom—both of which are in a permanent state of conflict. Too much of one means less of the other. Striking the balance between these phenomena is the true goal of the best policing.

The need for a formula
Societies in which principled policing operates, it is contended, are less likely to suffer from policing injustices than those where policing is driven by political opportunism, professional caprice or just bad law. There has to be a robust moral objectivity in the way in which policing operates if it is to avoid the worst misuses and abuses of power. To seek rationalisation of the police mission, and to give it coherence and form in both theory and practice, has always presented a personal challenge.

15

When leading and managing a major police organization by what is commonly called 'the seat of the pants', a good deal of luck and overwhelming power is required to avoid the worst results of such professional sin. On the other hand, consistency demands that command of policing and formation of policies is based on some coherent formula and framework. Such a formula provides not only consistency and objectivity, but is also available to other people for their understanding of the rationale of the behaviour behind policy-making. My own tried and tested formula was as follows:

1. **Philosophy** Through cogitation and reasoning to acquire an understanding of the police idea.
2. **Ideas** These are the product of 1 above
3. **Policies** Through the combination of 1 and 2—and through consultation—to fashion the directives, both operational and administrative, for the functioning of the organization.
4. **Performance** Through the use of power, and persuasion, to implement 3.

In this book I will seek to follow this formula, beginning with a review of some relevant philosophical theories.

PHILOSOPHY AND POLICING

I shall proceed on the reasonable assumption that philosophers have something important to teach people who work in the wider world of practical affairs. Specifically, in the present instance, the need is to address problems and uncertainties presented by the theory and practice of policing, and for their rationalisation. One ought not to underestimate the risks taken when engaging in critical comment on philosophical theories. Philosophers can not only be brutal with the intrepid interloper, but for their own kind they save the thrust of the intellectual dagger. Barely had the bones of the late Sir Karl Popper been laid to rest—and whilst the panegyrics for his life-time's contribution to the advance of knowledge and truth-seeking were still echoing around—when the following conclusions appeared in a respected journal:

> Popper preached the importance of open debate and recognition of error, but throughout his intellectual career he fought to insulate a discredited idea against any possible criticism. Perhaps it would be best now if we remember what Popper preached, and lay the rest of his doctrines quietly to rest. [2]

I shall be relying on Popper's insights here and there, since his world renowned work, *The Open Society and Its Enemies*, has, from my first reading of it, been an inspiration. Perhaps it is in the essential nature of philosophical debate that there can be no compromising what is considered to be the truth. 'Scientific truth' is always vulnerable to refutation, which is unsettling, and makes for difficulties. I do not profess to know.

The need for a philosophical base
Recourse to some philosophical justification of policing is essential in order to give a robust confidence to the police command, and thereby to the function, of the organization. Though it is easy to express this view, it is less easy to select and operate such principles in practice. The mysteries of philosophy sometimes resemble a movable feast, during which philosophers appear to be in permanent dispute. The 'high police' (see under the heading *High Police* later in this chapter for the definition of this term as used in this book) command has to bring to bear the experience and knowledge of practical worldly affairs which have their own unique legitimacy and strength.

I shall suggest that the high police should initially seek a philosophical basis for their police work in order that their thinking and actions may be rational. They will be aware, that as the coercive arm, they are part of government. They are therefore serving a political purpose, in which case political philosophies have direct relevance to their function.

It goes without saying that in a liberal democracy, whichever philosophy seems most apt should be moral and just, even at the expense of efficiency, but there are many police systems in the world where a different set of values and priorities apply. An extreme example of this would have been found in the work of the powerful political commissars under the communist system, whilst on the other hand, the police commander in a liberal democracy would be exposed to constant evaluation and criticism from any quarter. The police commander should of course seek efficiency, but not at any cost. In short, he or she is in search of a set of values of which they and all their officers should be aware, as well as what it is they are supposed to be protecting or defending. It is unlikely, though not impossible, that the values being sought are those already held by the commander, but in the main they are waiting to be discovered.

In the first place, those values which are exemplified by the political form of government and the social mores of the society which the police commander serves leave little room for novelty or idiosyncrasy, but this is not to say that the police cannot seek to ameliorate harsh injustice

17

under any system. In totalitarian systems it would be axiomatic to eschew the idea of freedom as a social value, even though there may be a certain amount of altruism. In a communist system privately owned property (for the police to protect) would not be regarded as high in value as would state property. In Britain the theft of public property is not regarded so seriously as is the theft of private property, as a general rule, e.g. 'It was only government cash', said a Scottish villager when he heard that his local Laird, an accountant at New Scotland Yard had stolen £5m.[3]

The French Declaration of the Rights of Man and the Citizen (26 August 1789) provides at article 2:

> The final end of every political institution is the preservation of the natural and imprescriptible rights of man. These rights are those of liberty, property, security and resistance to oppression.

At article 17, the Declaration describes property as 'an inviolable and sacred right . . .'. On the other hand, the Constitution (Fundamental Law) of the former Union of Soviet Socialist Republics (1936) Chapter X ('Fundamental Rights and Duties of Citizens') made no mention of ownership of private property; it provided at article 131 that 'It shall be the duty of every citizen of the USSR to safeguard and fortify public, socialist property, as the sacred and inviolable foundation of the Soviet system'. Thus a high police commander operating under the Soviet system would have had cause to assess the values by which he was obliged to act somewhat differently from his eighteenth century French counterpart.

A warning of the dangers

But then what is conscience? It may be that the political system in question, or part of it, seems to be unjust and unfair, or morally deficient, in which case a high police commander with equally high personal moral ethical standards would have to lower those standards to remain and serve the police organization, to fight against it from within (though there are obvious limits in confronting the political power behind the organization), or to resign.

It is a matter of record how the police are able to adjust to serving amoral political institutions, and this in turn reflects police culture and its reflexes to authoritarian command. Such a case is meticulously researched and portrayed by Christopher Browning in his book *Ordinary Men*.[4] This is a story of a battalion of German 'Order Police' recruited in Hamburg from the ranks of regular police officers and various tradesmen and skilled workers. In 1942 they were in Poland and under

18

the high police command of Heinrich Himmler and his SS lieutenants. They were non-combatants whose task was to police territory overrun and captured by the German Wehrmacht. As Browning says, they were 'ordinary men' and unlikely to represent a high concentration of men of violent predisposition. Yet the high police command was able to motivate more than 80 per cent of these men to engage in mass shootings of Jewish children, women and old men. Young men were used as slave labour. As its first operation the battalion was ordered to round up 1,800 Jews in Jozefow, 'the women, children and elderly were to be shot on the spot'. Reflecting on his part in the massacre, one policeman, formerly a sheet metal worker from Bremerhaven said:

> I made the effort, and it was possible for me, to shoot only children. It so happened that the mothers led the children by the hand. My neighbour then shot the mother and I shot the child that belonged to her, because I reasoned with myself that after all without its mother, the child could not live any longer. It was supposed to be, so to speak, soothing to my conscience to release children unable to live without their mothers.[5]

This is rationalisation of human brutality in the extreme.

THEORIES OF GOVERNMENT

We must now consider those theories of government which may give a rational meaning to the policing function. On the face of it, the principle that policing would contribute to 'the greatest happiness of the greatest number' of the people would seem to be attractive. But let us see what relevance the political theory of utilitarianism might have for our study of policing.

Utilitarianism and police

I began to think about utilitarianism following a conversation I once had with a respected lawyer who is a friend of mine and who was a clerk to a magistrates' court. He came upon me when I was reading a book and asked me what it was. I told him it was about capital punishment. He said that he supported such punishment and asked whether I did. I told him that I opposed it because there was always the possibility of executing someone who was innocent of the crime. His reply was 'Yes, but it doesn't happen often!' Something similar was allegedly said by a senior member of the English judiciary who expressed the opinion that capital punishment reduced the number of inquiries into miscarriages of justice; which, if not checked, could undermine public confidence in ('happiness with') the legal system! In both these instances injustices to individuals were being justified, or at least tolerated, to make society at large feel better, or happier. Now, was that so morally right?

Since my earlier studies of law, I have always been intrigued by the case of *R v Dudley and Stephens* (1884).[6] This well known incident is often cited as a test case for the defence of *necessity* in criminal law. Dudley, Stephens and someone called Brooks—who all had families—along with a 17-year-old cabin boy, had been shipwrecked 1,600 miles off the Cape of Good Hope. Having gone eight days without food, they realised that their only hope of survival was for one of them to be killed and eaten by the others. It is said, though it takes some believing, that the hapless cabin boy offered himself up for this purpose—and so was killed by Dudley and Stephens. They fed on the boy for eight days before being rescued and taken to Falmouth.

Eventually, their case came up at the Devon and Cornwall Assizes and was then transferred for trial at the High Court before five judges. During the trial Lord Coleridge, Chief Justice, quoting legal precedent, reminded the court that mere necessity was not in law a defence. He said:

> . . . if a person, being under necessity for want of victuals or clothes, and shall upon that account clandestinely and *animo furandi* steal another man's goods, it is a felony, and a crime by the laws of England, punishable with death.

He went on:

> . . . though the law and morality are not the same, and many things are immoral which are not necessarily illegal, yet the absolute divorce of law from morality would be of fatal consequence; and such divorce would follow if the temptation to murder in this case were to be held by the law to be an absolute defence of it.

Dudley and Stephens were sentenced to death—which was later commuted by the Crown to imprisonment for six months.

These incidents raise questions of the morality of the deeds done to individuals with a view to general happiness. Well now, my friend the clerk to the magistrates, and the Law Lord at the High Court, and the sailors who survived, conveniently thought that it was alright in certain circumstances to sacrifice one person's life if thereby you were saving the lives of some other people. But I find that hard to accept, not only in cases such as those to which I have referred, but as a general moral principle. This is a live issue in contemporary philosophy.[7]

20

Critics, it seems, share the opinion that when a plain man consults his conscience he will often find its deliverance at variance with those who are of the view that an act is right provided only that it will effect the greatest happiness of the greater number. As the philosopher Gertrude Anscombe pointed out, in certain conceivable circumstances utilitarianism could prescribe the execution of an innocent man.[8] It might be expedient that one man should die for the people, but as she says:

> If someone really thinks . . . that it is open to question whether such an action as procuring the judicial execution of the innocent should be quite excluded from consideration—I do not want to argue with him; he shows a corrupt mind.

The high police leader should be aware that the ethical theory of utilitarianism has its economic and political dimension described as 'the view of life presupposed in most modern and political and economic planning, when it is supposed that happiness is measured in economic terms'. But if police are not concerned with economic planning what aspects of the doctrine are of their direct concern? *The Oxford Dictionary of Philosophy*[9] records that 'the doctrine that applies utilitarianism to actions directly, so that an individual action is right if it increases happiness more than any alternative, is known as direct or act utilitarianism'.[10] In enforcing laws and restricting freedoms, it is not always immediately obvious that police activity is likely to increase anybody's happiness, though the protective role of the police may, and often does, reduce fear, and that is good; so in this sense it does increase happiness. Furthermore, society without some form of police, or with a form of police which is only concerned to serve and protect the freedom of an elite or privileged hegemony, would be infinitely worse than the utlitarian model, where the control of crime would undoubtedly add to the general happiness, though not at any price.

It is in the direct sense that police action may meet utilitarianism's demands because:

> Indirect versions apply in the first place to such things as institutions, systems of rules of conduct or human characters; these are best if they maximise happiness, and actions are judged only in so far as they are ordained by the institutions or systems, or rules, or those that would be performed by the person of optimal character.

Police therefore will have to be of the highest standards if they are to fulfil this demand of indirect utilitarianism, but we still need to reconcile the doctrine with concepts of justice and morality (discussed later in this chapter), and this seems to be no easy task.

It is commonly claimed that the utility principle enables us to resolve conflicts of obligation.[11] To be guided solely by intuition is perhaps too philosophically capricious, or inadequate, whilst utilitarianism offers an objective principle to show us what we ought to do. To reject the utilitarian principle, it is said, is to abandon the prospect of avoiding moral conflict. One modern moral philosopher[12] advocates a theory which it is claimed helps us to resolve such conflict. R. M Hare's 'two level' theory of moral thinking involves making decisions based on all the relevant 'logic and facts' available, and that what one feels one 'ought' to do should pass the test of universality, i.e. broadly to do the same in all similar cases. This 'prescriptivity' and 'universalisability' suffice to govern the reasoning behind moral thinking and judgments. Hare goes on to suggest that, under the right circumstances, his formula would be compatible with the utilitarian approach to moral problem solving, or in his own words, 'not inconsistent with utilitarianism'. He differentiates between what he calls respectively *intuitive* and *critical* thinking. Morality cannot do without concepts of right and wrong—its *intuitive* level. But since intuition lacks adequate objectivity, and in order to compensate for this, moral thinking has to take place at another level, namely, the *critical* level.

To throw light on the implications of Hare's theory I will quote W D Hudson:[13]

> Moral principles are of two kinds which may be described as *derived* and *underived* respectively. The underived kind are deliverances of a moral thinker's critical thinking. They are principles which he would not allow to be overridden in any conceivable circumstances. A moral thinker's principles of the derived kind by contrast, are the ones which he considers to be what Hare calls "acceptable utility". That is to say the thinker concerned considers that their general acceptance would be useful as a means to the fulfilment of his underived moral principles. To take the simplest of examples, suppose a moral thinker had arrived by critical thinking at the conclusion that we ought always to do what we think will maximise happiness. He might then consider if everyone told the truth except in abnormal circumstances, that would contribute significantly to the maximisation of happiness. In such a case, this moral thinkers' underived principle would be the maximization of happiness: and his derived principle, truth telling.

It seems that according to this theory the two levels of thinking reinforce each other in helping us to think our way out of moral dilemmas and conflicts, and, it is claimed, they are not unconcerned with utilitarianism. It is provided that the freedom to reason is fundamental to moral thinking. However, Hare's critics will not accept his theory of moral thinking. 'I do not believe that the styles of thought Hare seeks to describe could provide what his theories require', says Williams who believes that 'such thoughts are not stable under reflection'.[14]

Police after all need to have regard for the common good, and may at times therefore be required to make the greatest number unhappy in order to serve and protect a very small number, e.g. ethnic minorities, religious or political groups. In quite recent times, the minority nationalist community in Northern Ireland perceived the police to favour, support and serve the political majority—even where that majority perpetrated political and social distributive injustices upon them.[15] In this way the greatest number were happy, but a perceived denial of justice created such a high degree of unhappiness in the minority, that their violent reaction grew into a widespread terrorist campaign: '. . . we may know of the general impact institutions, rules and character have on the happiness of those affected by them'.

Making the greatest number of people happy through their feeling safe and free from the fear of crime, seems on the face of it to offer a reasonable enough police objective. But this says nothing about morality, and does the morality of policing not have anything to say?

The founder of the school of the political philosophy of utilitarianism, Jeremy Bentham (1748-1804), paid little heed to the work of Kant (1724-1804), and in particular to Kant's reputation as 'the philosophical defender par excellence of the right of man and his equality . . .'[16] Russell[17] tells us that Bentham had a great contempt for the doctrine of the rights of man. 'The rights of man', he said, 'are plain nonsense; the imprescriptable rights of man, nonsense on stilts'. But of particular interest to the high police is that 'Bentham's ideal, like that of Epicurus, was security not liberty'. I acknowledge that liberty is diminished when people feel afraid to exercise it, but to stress security to unnecessary extremes at the price of fundamental freedoms plays into the hands of would be high police despots. Such despots are quick to exploit fear in order to secure unlimited power. This seems to have characterised much of the rise of Hitler and his National Socialist Party in Germany in the 1930s.

The Nazi propaganda spoke of the communist party of the Weimar Republic as 'The Red Terror'. Police raids were carried out on offices, and on the communist HQ in Berlin on 24 February 1933. A purported discovery of plans for a communist revolution was calculated to strike apprehension in the minds of thinking people. When the Reichstag building 'mysteriously' went up in flames on the night of February 27, it only intensified public fear, and provided the pretext for government by decree, in order to assuage the public desire for security. The day after the fire, Hitler promulgated a decree signed by the President 'for the

23

protection of the people and the state'. The decree was described 'as a defensive measure against communist acts of violence'.[18] It began by suspending the guarantees of individual liberty under the Weimar Constitution.

Thus: restrictions on personal liberty; on the right of free expression of opinion (including freedom of the press); on the right of assembly and association; violations of the privacy of postal, telegraph and telephonic communications; warrants for house searches; and orders for confiscation—as well as restrictions on property were *permissible beyond the legal limits otherwise prescribed.*

In addition to the decree, very heavy penalties (life imprisonment or execution) were provided for political crimes. This cameo of political tyranny plays on fear and then takes away liberty. This is not to suggest that utilitarianism intends such behaviour, but that the central place of human rights in modern politics may not be compatible with the doctrine. Protective security has still to grapple with the conundrum of maximising freedoms and at the same time controlling disorder, and this calls for great skill and determination.

If the modern high police leader needs to understand a more contemporary view of utilitarianism in relation to morality, he or she must seek out more recent pronouncements on the subject. In his book *Morality: An Introduction to Ethics*, Bernard Williams,[19] after considering the theory, concludes devastatingly

> . . . if utilitarianism is true, and some fairly plausible empirical propositions are also true, then it is better that people should not believe in utilitarianism. If, on the other hand, it is false, then it is certainly better that people should not believe in it. So, either way, it is better that people should not believe in it.

Sabine wrote of 'the grim egoism of utilitarian ethics, and of classical economics'.[20] Considering the greatest happiness principle which prescribed that 'the only rational guide both to private morals and to public policy' was that of the greatest happiness of the greatest number, it is not difficult to agree with Sabine. But it is to John Rawls and his 'justice as fairness' theory that I turn for more recent consideration of the subject. In comparing and contrasting utilitarianism with social contract doctrine (see later in this chapter), Rawls says that 'utilitarianism may seem to be a more exalted ideal, but the other side of it is that it may authorise the lesser welfare and liberty of some for the sake of a greater happiness of others who may already be more fortunate'.[21]

I have already pointed to the seeming moral weakness in the doctrine, and Rawls goes on to express his belief thus:

... however improbable the congruence of the right and the good in "justice as fairness" it is surely more probable than on the utilitarian view. The conditional balance of reasonableness favours the contract doctrine.

Rawls maintains that classical utilitarianism fails to take seriously the distinction between persons and is thereby flawed in terms of his own theory.

The theory of protectionism

In his critique of Plato's *Politics*, Karl Popper unearths a theory which he calls 'protectionism'.[22]

> Aristotle tells us that Lycophron (c 400 BC) considered the law of the state as a "covenant by which men assure one another of justice". He tells us that Lycophron looked upon the state as an instrument for the protection of its citizens against acts of injustice (and for permitting them peaceful intercourse, especially exchange), demanding that the state be a "cooperative association for the prevention of crime".

As we shall see this appears to adumbrate a theory of the state which was later to be described as a contract. The theory called 'protectionism' seems to offer much for the high police leader.

Popper was of the opinion[23] that in this quest for a theory of the state we should not begin by asking 'What is the state, its nature and meaning?' or 'How did it originate?', and so on. He poses, then answers his own rhetorical questions. 'What do we demand from the state? What do we propose to consider the legitimate aim of state activity? Why do we prefer living in a well ordered state, to living without a state, i.e. in anarchy?' He believes this 'to be a rational way of asking this question, and that it is a question which a technologist must try to answer, for only if he knows what he wants can he decide whether a certain institution is o: is not well adapted to its function'. Now this is the very question fa ing the high police official when seeking to discover whether a pɛ ·ticular police institution is well adapted to producing a well ordered so iety.

A humanitarian (and we hope that our high police officials *are* hu nanitarians) might answer: 'What I demand from the state is prc :ection; not only for myself but for others too. I demand protection for ny own freedom and for other people's. Now I am glad to say that this is one case where the humanitarian philosopher's theory of protection is, by happy coincidence, the same as mine was when I was a high police practitioner. In practice however it is not easy to convince police practitioners that they are to protect an abstraction such as 'freedom' or 'liberty'. But when speaking of freedom Popper wants us to know that he is ready to have his own freedom curtailed by the state, provided the freedom which remains is protected by the state. Thus, 'The fundamental purpose of the state' should be 'the protection of that freedom which does not harm other citizens'. And furthermore, any limitations put on the freedom of citizens should be put on as equally as possible. I agree with this entirely and as a high police practitioner sought to ensure that this principle was well understood by those for whom I was responsible. It is of great help to the high police leaders when fashioning their policies to have a theory permitting a rational approach to political challenge, i.e. from the point of view of a fairly clear and definite aim. The theory we are discussing is characterised by the qualities of equalitarianism, individualism, and protectionism against injustice; but in one of his more combative moods, Popper, in attacking Plato's theory of justice, sums up by saying 'We can say that Plato's theory of justice, as presented in the *Republic* and later works, is a conscious attempt to get the better of the equalitarian, individualistic, and protectionist tendencies of his time, and to re-establish the claims of tribalism by developing a totalitarian moral theory . . . and . . . in the case of the totalitarian class rule of a naturally superior master race'.[24]

If we are to follow Popper's analysis here, it is the high police of the totalitarian state who may have more to gain from Plato than have those of liberal democracies, for whom Lycophron's protectionist contract should be the beacon.

Social contract theory and the police

I mentioned earlier that the theory of protectionism adumbrated the subsequent development of the social contract theory. In what sense, if any, might it be said that policing can be described in social contractual terms? In embarking upon an examination of the relevant theory and its pertinence for policing, I must make it clear at the outset that I accept without demur the adverse criticism of the historicist theory of the social contract as offered for example, by Hume and others. That is to say, the refutation of the idea that in natural law there existed in the mists of time, beyond which the memory of man runneth not, an original agreement between ruler and ruled. However, in a politically developed and plural society, political ideas, nuances and a vocabulary are necessary to progress. It is the notion of an *implied* contract, rather than the existence of an *original* contract arising from some historical binding agreement, that is worthy of its place in our political thinking. It is not necessary to rehearse the arguments of those theorists who in the past had to contend with the power of myths such as the divine right of kings. It is enough to accept that 'as a legal fiction to justify government, the theory of the social contract has some measure of truth'.[25]

In Kantian terms the original contract is not a principle explaining either the origin of civil society or the state; but rather the principle of political government which deals with ideals of legislation and legal justice as well as administration. The high police person facing this situation is searching for principles with which to explain such a purpose to those in his organization.

The question of moral purpose will need to be addressed in due course. What must presently be addressed is the notion that a contractual relationship—in one form or another—exists in most, if not in all societies between persons *inter se*, and between individuals and individuals and between individuals and those who exercise power of government over them.

In the 1994 United States Congressional elections, the Republican Party published its manifesto, 'Republican Contract with America', in which it promised to do many things if elected. These included the 'Taking Back Our Streets Act'; 'An Anti-crime Package' including stronger truth-in-sentencing, 'good faith' exclusionary rule exemptions, effective death penalty provisions, and 'cuts in social spending from this summers "crime" bill to fund prison construction and additional law enforcement to keep people secure in their neighbourhoods and kids safe in their schools'. The statement concluded with these words: 'Respecting the judgment of our fellow citizens, we seek their mandate for reform, we hereby pledge our names to this "contract with America"'.

Around the same time as the US case, the various parties involved in the Algerian political crisis were meeting in Rome in order to seek a way out of a bloody impasse which agonised Algerian society. The Algerian delegates published the results of their findings for a pathway to peace and order in the country, which they called 'A Platform for a Peaceful Political Solution of Algeria's Crisis; or a National Contract'. This document includes sections on 'Framework; values and principles'; 'Rejection of violence as a means of acceding, or maintaining power'; and it deals with issues of political pluralism, universal suffrage, and other political items.[26]

Though some philosophers dispute the theoretical basis for the social contract, nevertheless acceptance of the idea as being some form of 'legal fiction' is of political utility when discussing and carrying on government. Thus it would seem from the United States and Algerian examples quoted above that the vocabulary of politics finds ready use for the language and meaning of the social contract theory. In his famous work, *Ancient Law*, Sir Henry Maine[27] referred to what philosophers called the social contract as a theory 'which, though nursed into importance by political passions, derived all its sap from speculation of

27

lawyers'. He goes on to castigate some political philosophers, notably Rousseau, and particularly the idea that man, in a state of nature, had achieved the 'social compact as a historical fact'. I agree with Maine on this, and am prepared to view the theory as 'an ingenious hypothesis, or a convenient verbal formula'.

The high police person would be aware of the nature of the law of contract and the idea that obligations are imposed upon the parties to it. More explicitly it is one of my main concerns to stress the importance of moral obligations and liabilities arising from the social contract theory as we assess them for their relevance to policing. Maine ascribes it all to the genius of Roman law. He believes that 'the positive duty resulting from one man's reliance on the word of another, is amongst the slowest conquests of advancing civilisation', and that 'the movement of progressive societies has hitherto been a movement from status to contract'.[28] As police come to understand the Kantian doctrine of dignity of the person, it may be to mutual advantage to accede to the notion that the people upon whom they exercise their power, or those for whom they are exercising it, stand in the kind of implied contractual relationship which calls for moral ethical standards of behaviour, with which to characterise the exercise of their legal powers.

So far we have discovered a political theory of a contractual nature which calls for the state, and we may add civil society, where it exists, to be a 'cooperative association for the prevention of crime', and to regard the law of the state as a 'covenant by which men assure one another of justice'—and all this to be characterised by dimensions of equalitarianism and individualism. It is at this juncture that the high police have to face what is meant by the term 'justice'. But before considering this, we should not leave social contract theory without giving an opportunity to Popper to explain why he believes a social contract theory in Lycophron's terms (p. 25) 'is the most fitting expression of the humanitarian and equalitarian movement of the Periclean age'.[29]

It is a contract theory which is secure from the objections to which the historicist theory is exposed, and this is because in the first place Lycophron makes no mention of the idea that a contract existed according to natural law. If Maine is right (above), then the concept of 'a contract' had not yet been developed by the Roman lawyers, which he believes gave politicians the notion which they later exploited.

Lycophron's protectionist theory—being equalitarian and individualistic—offended Plato's theory of society based on class, and according to Popper 'We have been robbed of it'. Protectionism is not a selfish theory, since it applies to each and every person, and not to self-protection only. To protect the weak from being bullied by the strong is a

28

moral obligation with contractual implications, and if Popper is right, as surely he must be, then principled policing has a moral obligation to the protectionist theory, and is obliged by social contractual terms to carry it out. We shall notice further revival of support for the social contract theory when we come to consider modern versions in the works of John Rawls under *Justice as fairness* (p. 30)

JUSTICE

I was once confronted by the ire of a judge of the High Court of England and Wales who rejected anything to do with metaphysical notions such as 'justice'. To say that I was astonished would be to put it mildly. Perhaps he was of the school of legal positivism, which—whilst having its adherents—is not what I would imagine a high police officer in pursuit of the wider social and moral sensitivities surrounding the policing function to be looking for. The idea of 'justice' has to be considered very carefully and seriously by high police officials responsible for enlightening members of their organization concerning criminal justice. Would a society, or part of it, being denied distributive justice present more problems for policing? There is plenty of historical evidence that it would. The very roots of terrorism within a state can often be traced to distributive injustices.

Minority rights denied through discrimination on racial, ethnic, or religious grounds are the most common causes of terrorism to combat which the high police have to develop policies and strategies which rely on force, and sometimes on Draconian legal measures. These measures have included detention without trial, criminal courts without juries, forcible restriction and geographical confinement, and internal exile. The whole dreadful saga of the *Gulag Archipeligo* of the Soviet Union under Stalin is so eloquently and passionately portrayed by Alexander Solzhenitsyn is his voluminous work of that name. Such extreme police measures amount to injustice rather than to justice. But what is 'justice'? 'This question can be just as perplexing for a jurist as the well-known question "What is the truth?" is for the logician . . . '[30]

There are numerous answers (and much sophistry) to this question, which has occupied philosophers from Plato to the present time, with differing results. The policeman is not only concerned with what *is called* criminal justice, but also with what *amounts to* criminal injustice. To begin with we need to define the subject, and to do so I again intend to draw on the work of John Rawls[31] whose modern treatment of it is comprehensive and respected. High police should have regard to his work in which he describes justice as fairness, and the first virtue of social institutions. Much of his philosophy is sympathetic to the social contract theory of government.

Justice as fairness[32]

At the outset it must be made clear that John Rawls's theory of justice as fairness is the result of lengthy and voluminous exposition, and that any attempt to reduce it to a short commentary cannot work. It is worthy of note, however, that he throws down the gauntlet to the utilitarians in the name of justice as fairness, and this alone is an important episode in moral philosophy. Rawls insists that justice in the widest sense of the meaning of the term is the first claim on governmental institutions, and this concept conflicts at the outset with the utilitarian idea that all that matters is the greatest happiness of the greatest number. People live in society in a relationship contractual in form which insists on the moral criteria of rights and duties. But in spite of not being able to treat Rawls in a comprehensive way, it is very important to take notice here of his two principles of justice[33] for institutions, since policing of a society requires that when social strategies and public order are under consideration, these principles concerning justice as fairness might be brought into use.

The First Principle is that each person shall have an equal right to the most extensive total system of equal basic liberties compatible with a system of liberty for all. (An understanding of the social implications of this First Principle is required by High Police, since it is not only morally correct under the equalitarian principle, but those societies which are in blatant disregard of it face problems of social unrest and potential, or actual, disorder).

The Second Principle concerns social and economic inequalities, and Rawls' attempt to justify those which are inevitable, and how to deal with those which are not. It is his 'Priority Rules' which have the greatest relevance for police.

His First Priority Rule requires that the principles of justice are to be ranked in lexical order, and therefore liberty can be restricted only for the sake of liberty (cf. Kant and Popper). There are two cases: (a) a less extensive liberty must strengthen the total system of liberty shared by all; (b) a less than equal liberty must be acceptable to those with lesser liberty. Situation (a) would cover judicial imprisonment of the dangerous; and situation (b) the voluntary restrictions accepted in the private lives of those belonging to organizations such as the police, military, religious orders, and so on.

Rawl's Second Priority Rule (The Priority of Justice Over Efficiency and Welfare) is primarily concerned with the distribution of economic and other goods, but as a principle it can have relevance to the policing of a society in that justice cannot be sacrificed in the cause of efficient criminal investigation and prosecution.

Finally it is worthy of note that what Rawls calls the general conception means 'all social and primary goods—liberty and opportunity, income and wealth, and the bases of self respect—are to be distributed equally, unless an unequal distribution of any or all of these goods is to the advantage of the least favoured.' All this seems to differ from the social morality of utilitarianism.

Rawl's formula calls for a situation in which policing policies reflect the paramouncy of liberty rather than the priority of power. Power should only be applied to enhance liberty, and the liberty of a few may have to be restricted for the freedom of the many provided that such arrangements comply with the equalisation principle. This would apply, e.g. to requirements to drive on one side of the road to avoid doing harm to others. A more controversial restriction of liberty in the United States would be to diminish the liberty to possess firearms (a right under the Constitution) since privately held firearms damage the liberties of many innocent victims, thus denying their freedom.

The ideal situation for police is one in which they are able to operate in a just manner in a just society. If operating in what is generally a just society it is possible, to some extent, to ameliorate a degree of injustice by using discretion (in those police systems which permit some discretion: for some *do not*), and not enforcing laws generally regarded as unjust, e.g. through desuetude (or 'lapse'). Care has to be taken, however, not to be in neglect of duty through failing to fulfil the will of the legislature. This is a difficult line for the police, and it should be trodden with great care. High police officials will realise that the repeal or amendment of archaic and unjust laws is a matter for the political process. The situation presents a moral dilemma. In a liberal democracy, police may not take an active role in the politics of parties. Police can only justify involvement in law reform through constitutional channels, and particularly where unjust laws are considered to be in conflict with the constitution.

A practical example: Justice versus efficiency?

Police are sometimes presented with an opportunity to exert pressure on the system of laws by putting them to the test; this is particularly the case where the law may be uncertain. Such an opportunity presented itself to me in 1981. I need not dwell on the case at length since it is fully dealt with in two law reports, and legal textbooks.[34]

The Central Electricity Generating Board, a nationalised body sought to test a site within my jurisdiction for a nuclear power station. Peaceful protests ensued, and the farmers owning the land, and who had objected to this exploration, were neutralised by being served with High Court injunctions, as were many local residents. Other protesters arrived from elsewhere and obstructed the vehicles and machinery of the board on what was private land, the owners of which did not declare them to be trespassers. The board sought to persuade me, and my officers—as constables with the power—to arrest the protesters, deeming them to be in breach of the criminal law. I refused to do this on the grounds that I was exercising my *discretion* not to arrest as the law was not clear. Subsequent appeals to the High Court and later the Court of Appeal for an order of *mandamus* failed. In effect, the board were told to exercise their own powers at common law, which they declined to do. Although the entire operation lasted for six months no-one was arrested, injured or assaulted. Had the police taken a more heavy handed approach to this situation, injustice and anger could well have been aroused. It seems that this is a situation fitting Rawls' principle of liberty, where justice comes before efficiency.

Distributive and retributive justice

I think it important for high police to address the question of the two justices, namely *distributive* and *retributive* justice, and their relationship. Rawls stresses—and I fully accept both the logic of his position and its relevance to my practical experience—that the basic structure of society and the way in which major social institutions should provide for fundamental rights and duties is the key to distributive justice, and to prospects of keeping the peace. After all, 'in justice as fairness society is interpreted as a cooperative venture for mutual advantage' (see p. 25 for Popper's account of Lycophron's demand that the state be a 'co-operative association for the prevention of crime'), and any markedly unjust distribution of fundamental social assets tends to vitiate the social contract involved. Once freed from the moral obligation of mutual cooperation, behaviour which is inimical to a well-ordered society is, from experience, predictable, and police contingency planners would be well advised to understand this, and to warn governments accordingly. The high police leader will need to consider any relationship there may be between retributive and distributive justice, since distributive injustice, if marked and obvious, may lead to public disorder, crime, insurrection, and even to terrorism. One only has to read daily newspapers, or listen to news reports, to find confirmation of the truth of this. Rawls says:

> It is true that in a reasonably well-ordered society those who are punished for violating just laws have normally done something wrong. Of course, such a society like any society, has to have a system of punishment for wrong-doing in order to uphold basic natural dues.

The distribution of social and economic goods is another matter, 'the arrangements are not the converse so to speak, of the criminal law so just that the one punishes certain offences, the other rewards moral worth'.[35] Criminal justice is not fully realisable since it admits of the acquittal of the guilty, and from time to time conviction of the innocent, since the system can only arrive at decisions through the evidence and rules constructed for its purpose; it must always remain flawed and imperfect. This is what Rawls describes as a 'partial compliance' theory. There is no such fundamental flaw in the theory of distributive justice which 'belongs to strict compliance theory and so to consideration of the ideal.'

Kant, or Kantian justice and police

Kant is very helpful to the police where he addresses the questions of the use of coercion, and of justice.[36] Coercion is, after all, a central purpose (not the only one) of the police arm of the state, or government.

> Now everything that is unjust is a hindrance to freedom, according to universal laws. Coercion however is a hindrance or opposition to freedom. Consequently, if a certain use of freedom is itself a hindrance to freedom according to univerals laws [that is, is unjust] then the use of coercion to counteract it, in as much as it is the prevention of hindrance to freedom, is consistent with freedom according to universal laws; in other words, this use of coercion is just. It follows by the law of contradiction that justice [a right] is united with the authorisation to use coercion against anyone who violates justice [or a right].

This equates with Popper's comment (see p. 25) noted earlier, that the fundamental purpose of the state (and therefore police) should be the protection of that freedom which does not harm other citizens. When we set this test against police excesses which around the world deny freedom, we are able to talk of police as either handmaidens of justice or of injustice. The high police have to face this—they are either just, and therefore morally to be approved of—or unjust, and to be morally condemned. This point has to be taken one step further to the stage where any restrictions on freedom, which pass the preceding test of just coercion, must be applied equally, or if applied unequally, would have passed the test of just coercion in design, only to fail as unjust in its application.

THE RULE OF LAW

At this stage, it may occur to the enquirer that freedom is dependent on the Rule of Law. In order to consider this, we need to ask 'What is the

Rule of Law?'—since we have already noted that laws may be unjust for various reasons, or though just in themselves they may be unjustly enforced, e.g. with partiality.

In considering whether coercive police action is moral therefore— even when it accords with the so called 'Rule of Law'—we need further clarification of what might be a legal rule which is morally just. In English constitutional law, according to Dicey,[37]

> ... it means in the first place the absolute supremacy or predominance of the regular law as opposed to the influence of arbitrary power, and excludes the existence of arbitrariness, or prerogative or even of wide discretionary authority on the part of government.

This principle should motivate police to defend freedom through laws, since to do otherwise is to act unjustly and unconstitutionally. Dicey's second point is that the Rule of Law

> ... means, again, equality before the law, or the equal subjection of all classes to the ordinary law of the land administered by the ordinary law courts.

This ensures that police and other public officials, are not exempt from the duty of obedience to the same laws as are other citizens.

Dicey's last point is a formula for expressing that the laws of the constitution (which in some countries are part of a constitutional code) in Great Britain '... are not the source but the consequence of the rights of individuals as defined and enforced by the courts'. But this is not enough. Dicey leaves us short of the idea of the *justice* and *morality* of laws. After all, there may be a duty of civil disobedience as a moral reflex to unjust laws, and this places great strain on the morality of the police function.

According to Fuller,[38] there is what he would describe as the 'inner morality of law' and he goes on to argue for the Rule of Law to be prospective in its effect (not retrospective legislation making past actions into new crimes); that laws should be extant, comprising general rules, but not vague (people have to know what laws are saying if they are to comply); that laws should embody constancy and not caprice; that they should be capable of being complied with (so as not to punish people for failing to do the impossible); and lastly, that police and other government officials stand in the same position in relation to laws as do the general public.

34

The high police official in the Federal Republic of Germany would know that article 1 of the Constitution of that Republic concerns the protection of human dignity, viz:

> The dignity of man should be inviolable. To respect and protect it shall be the duty of all state authority.

Now the police leader would have a duty to translate the idea of the Rule of Law, and the dignity of the individual into policies for the direction and conduct of police. But it is no longer sufficient to regard the Rule of Law as restricted to the domestic state. International law requires that police officials comply with certain international treaties and conventions which in some parts of the world, notably those countries belonging to the Council of Europe, have as strong a duty to the rule of law embodying the Convention of Human Rights as to their domestic laws. The European Convention of Human Rights and Fundamental Freedoms requires that states which are parties to the convention must acknowledge the jurisdiction of the European Commission and the European Court and of the Council of Europe—and this body of law is designed to produce certain standards of behaviour affecting police as well as other governmental officials (see *Chapter 3* for further discussion about human rights).

HIGH POLICE

So far we have been concerned with various strands of philosophical theories in order to seek rationalisation of, and principles for, the policing of a just and moral society. We have not yet considered policing practice. Before concluding this chapter therefore, we might take note of five major historical high police practitioners, not for their exemplary police practice, but as examples, mainly notorious, of policemen who have occupied the pinnacle of power in contrasting political situations. Supreme police power, given the opportunity, can produce the most debased and debasing of human institutions. It is a power which need not be fettered into impotence, but which must be bound by the highest of principles, if it is to be regarded as morally worthy.

Throughout this book, the use of the term 'high police' is not to be confused with the old French usage, which meant those aspects of police which kept a close watch on plotters, and political machinations against high society. In the aftermath of the French Revolution—as is the tendency following all revolutions—counter-revolutionaries posed a potential threat which offered scope for a powerful minister of police like

Fouché, Duc d'Ortranto (1759-1820) who it is said saw his role as 'policing internal politics'.

Believing that the monarchy failed in 1789 '. . . through the nullity of high police', he said:

> The minister himself had to get in contact with the outstanding and influential men of all opinions, all doctrines, all superior classes of society. This system always succeeded with me, and I knew the secret France better from oral and confidential communications and from untrammelled talk than from the hotch potch of writings that passed under my eyes. Thus nothing essential to the security of the state ever escaped me.[39]

High police today, in the Fouché sense, are to be found in the secret and political police, sometimes described as security services. In our case the expression 'high police' is used to denote those with power to make and to implement policies affecting a police organization as a whole.

Five case studies of high police

Two of the following cases are products of post-revolutionary societies, one of a totalitarian coup, and two of western democracies.

Fouché

Joseph Fouché was born near Nantes France in 1765 and died in Trieste Italy in 1820. He was educated by the Oratorians, a Christian religious order, and for a while he was a priest and a teacher. Nothing here to suggest he would become a butcher of people and a scheming 'high' policeman. By the age of 30, Fouché had become a member of the revolutionary movement known as the Jacobins, and was elected to the National Convention. He was soon to be noticed vigorously demanding the execution of King Louis XVI, and the extinction of Christianity in France. It fell to his lot to execute the terrorists' vengeance of the Convention on the people of the city of Lyon who had revolted against the Jacobins and the revolution. As the death toll of the executed mounted, his reaction was summed up in his cynical comment 'Death is but an eternal sleep'. Intrigue and duplicity in the highest degree marked his career as he avoided being consumed by the terror of which he was such a major party. He had, after all, played a leading role in bringing about the downfall and execution of his fellow Jacobin, Robespierre.

There is no doubt that his skill and energy made him such a powerful figure in post-revolutionary France that—following brief periods as ambassador in Milan and the Hague—in July 1779 he became what he is best remembered for in European police lore, the minister of police. When Napoleon returned from Egypt in October 1779, Fouché

36

had already intrigued and plotted his rise to the top of the pyramid of power. He now began to elevate the role of the police. 'I felt', he wrote, 'that all the daring, the skill of a statesmenlike minister should be absorbed in "high police" and that what was left could safely be handed to heads of department'.[40] We see here the idea of the police state. Fouché placed the high police at the heart of the imperial police system. The high police were

> the regulating power which is felt everywhere, without ever being seen, and which, at the centre of the state holds the place which the power which sustains the harmony of the celestial bodies holds in the universe, a power whose regularity strikes although we are unable to divine the cause. Every branch of the administration has a part which subordinates it to the police.[41]

It was this model and example of police which made it so difficult for a near British contemporary, Sir Robert Peel. to get his English police reforms through the Houses of Parliament. Fouché, by now a wealthy man, died in alienation in Trieste where he was domiciled. He died in bed, which is more than can be said for some of our examples of high police.

Sir Robert Peel [42]

Robert Peel, a near contemporary of Fouché, was only 24-years-old when appointed Chief Secretary of Ireland in 1812. He was the son of a Lancashire cotton manufacturer, and a politician in the Tory ranks. He was a member of parliament for an Irish constituency. It was in Ireland that he was faced with the problems of necessary police reforms to take over the task of peace-keeping from the military. There was a constant threat of insurrection against British rule by the Irish peasantry. He called for a Peace Preservation Police which later became the police model in other British colonies. It was in his capacity as home secretary for England and Wales, that Peel's fame as a high police reformer was established.

Since the time of King Alfred the Great (871-900), the English had established a peace keeping system based on responsibilities of local communities. Such was the antipathy towards a strong central and political police machine that a Parliamentary committee—set up in 1822 by Peel to consider police reforms—reported to the effect that, in spite of crime and public disorder, they preferred to put up with this rather than the establishment of a police force which threatened the 'freedom of action and exemption from interference, which are the great privileges and blessings of society in this country'.

37

Through astute political acumen and the support of the prime minister, then the Duke of Wellington, Peel was able to establish a police force for London in 1829, and which subsequently influenced policing throughout the Anglo-Saxon world.

One of Peel's greatest services to police reform was the establishing of police principles which have stood the test of time. In the beginning he had no political police or plain clothes detectives as these were not politically acceptable. It was in 1829 that his enlightened views, which have characterised many advanced democratic police systems since that time, were set-down as follows:

> It should be understood at the outset that the object to be attained is the prevention of crime. To this great end every effort of the police is to be directed. The security of the person and property, and the preservation of a police establishment, will thus be better effected than by the detection and punishment of the offender after he has succeeded in committing crime. . .

> He [the constable] will be civil and obliging to all people of every rank and class.

> He must be particularly cautious not to interfere idly or unnecessarily in order to make a display of his authority; when required to act, he will do so with decision and boldness; on all occasions he may expect to receive the fullest support in the proper exercise of his authority. He must remember that there is no qualification so indispensable to a police officer as a perfect command of temper, never suffering himself to be moved in the slightest degree by any language or threats which might be used; if he does his duty in a quiet and determined manner such conduct will probably excite the well-disposed of bystanders to assist him, if he requires them.

It was on these foundation principles that police in England and Wales became established. They are an example of the timelessness of police principles for a liberal, democratic and civilised society—and point to the genius of the high police administration of Sir Robert Peel. In this way was the ethos of succeeding generations of police established.

There is a suggestion in the foregoing principles that provided the police act properly they may expect to receive 'the fullest support', and that 'well-disposed bystanders' would assist them. All of this suggests reciprocal obligations which characterise some form of social contract.

Lavrentii Beria[43]

Our next example of high police is Lavrentii Beria who, in another post-revolutionary state, the USSR, became the powerful chief of police apparatus, and later minister, or Peoples' Commissar for Internal Affairs.

Like Fouché, Beria (1899-1953) was a young man (19-years-old) when the revolution started, and like Fouché, because of his youth, he carried little political baggage to embarrass his high police ambitions. By the age of 39, he had plotted, schemed, and eliminated rivals to such a degree that Stalin, a fellow Georgian, made him his trusted Chief of NKVD (Peoples' Commissar) in 1938.

Amy Knights, in her excellent book, *Beria: Stalin's First Lieutenant*, says: 'Beria has long symbolised all the evils of Stalinism'. Stalin called him 'Our Himmler' (of whom see later in this chapter) in an exchange with Roosevelt at Yalta. Knights also reveals that the astute and intelligent Beria was just as important to Stalin as Himmler was to Hitler, if not more so! At the peak of his powers, Beria was responsible for all intelligence, counter-intelligence and domestic security. He also commanded the vast slave labour network of the GULAG (see Solzhenitsyn's *One Day in the Life of Ivan Denisovich*). He eventually took charge of the Soviet nuclear bomb project. Sir Karl Popper told me that Andrei Sakharov, the soviet nuclear physicist, was 'the most dangerous man who ever lived', since he provided the most powerfully destructive nuclear bombs imaginable for Beria, and later Khruschev at the time of the Cuban crisis. Andrei Sakharov recalls that when Beria offered him his 'slightly moist and deathly cold hand', he began to realise that he was 'face to face with a terrifying human being'. [44]

Beria had undoubtedly been responsible for the most cruel, brutal even fiendish behaviour. In his quest for power, and through purges, he was the cause of countless numbers of people being 'liquidated'. He was obviously feared by his rivals, including Khruschev. [45] 'I was shocked by his two faced scheming hypocrisy', and 'Stalin once even confided to me his own unhappiness with Beria's influence'. He went on: 'Anyone who wanted to be sure of staying in Stalin's good graces had to fawn all over Beria too. His arrogance and his treachery grew in direct proportion to his increasingly powerful position'; and '. . . he was skilful at anything that was filthy and treacherous'.

Khruschev tells us that Bulganin did not trust Beria either. It is irony that, after the death of Stalin, Beria should have worked for some amelioration of Stalinist excesses to the point where he became the victim of intrigue himself. He had made too many enemies in high places. Khruschev was most condemnatory. On 26 June 1953, Beria was arrested. New details of all this have recently emerged. His trial before a political tribunal was held in camera. He was shot.

Heinrich Himmler

Himmler (1900-1945) was the protagonist of the pernicious doctrines of 'Herrenvolk' and 'Untermenschen'. An archytypal 'ethnic cleanser', he took the coward's way out when faced with arrest and trial, and the hell which he had predominantly created. He bit on a cyanide capsule.

Himmler was born in Munich into a devout catholic house, the son of a social climbing professor and the grandson of a Bavarian police sergeant. He took an early interest in politics. The historian Peter Padfield[46] describes his interest in Jewish affairs when he was 25 years of age, but he was not then a fanatic, and he had growing doubts about the church. He was proud of the fact that when he had taken five cuts in a duel at his college, as he noted in his diary, 'I really did not flinch once'. He was 28 when he took over the infant SS which was subsequently to dominate the Nazi Party and the entire German nation. In his story of the SS, Heinz Holne[47] describes Himmler's adulation of Hitler whom he ridiculously described as 'The greatest brain of all time'.

His vision (with that of Heidrich) of creating a police state and becoming Germany's supreme policeman, drove him from being head of the Bavarian police, and Political Police, to becoming Reichsfuhrer SS, and chief of all German police; he was by then 36. His power struggle *en route* included outwitting Herman Goring, President of the Prussian police, by amalgamating his command with the entire national police machine. From this point onwards the totalitarian police state of the German Third Reich, and all its horrors, was to follow.[48]

The story of the SS is painstakingly researched and described by Heinz Hohne in his comprehensive account, *The Order of the Death's Head*. Of all the high police, the reign of Himmler, from age 36 to 45, surely must account for more degradation of the human species than any other of his high police rivals, or perhaps any other person in history. In 1944 at the peak of his power he commanded the Nazi police juggernaut of some million of personnel, from its military arm of the Waffen SS to the Einsatzgruppen of the concentration camps—the liquidators. It is the story of a very 'ordinary' man, and as amazing as it is appalling.

> As a loyal soldier I had to obey, for no state can survive without obedience and discipline. It rests with me alone to decide how long I still have to live (sic) since my life has now become meaningless. And what will history say of me? Petty minds, bent on revenge, will hand down a false and perverted account of the great and the good things I have accomplished for Germany. (April 1945: Himmler to his Swedish chiropractor, Kersten).[49]

Arrested by the British, but due to his disguise as a sergeant in uniform, not recognised, Himmler, as Chaim Herzog recalls, could easily have passed for a small, anonymous clerk. Finally identified, he crushed his phial of potassium cyanide between his teeth.

J Edgar Hoover

Meanwhile back in Washington DC, USA, America's own democratic version of high police power was grappling with his own enemies, including the wife of the ailing President (Eleanor Roosevelt), as well as the 'enemies' of his country. J. Edgar Hoover, the first and long serving director of the Federal Bureau of Investigation, had reached the zenith of his powers when 'all Congressmen and Senators are afraid of him', (Harry S Truman, President of the USA, in a letter to his wife, September 1947).[50]

The son of a stonemason, J. Edgar Hoover (1895-1972) was born in Washington DC in 1895 into a religious family. 'He never outgrew their Victorian manners and mores; that righteous Christian sensibility not only remained with him throughout his life but was the fuse for his complex personality'.[51] (Both Fouché and Himmler began life in similar religious circumstances, though they both abandoned their religion in spectacular fashion. Beria's mother was very religious also, but her son found his religion in Bolshevikism).

For almost 50 years from 1925 Hoover held virtually unchecked public power. By any standards he was a successful director in his own business of investigating federal crimes, but along the way he manipulated almost every President from Franklin Roosevelt to Richard Nixon. It was strange that he seemingly shrank from human contact. 'He used illegal wire taps and hidden mikes to destroy anyone who opposed him'.[52] According to the numerous comments made to the author by FBI agents, Hoover ruled them with a ruthlesness and frequent injustice which made strong men quake.

At his peak he helped to create McCarthyism, blackmailed the Kennedy brothers and even influenced the Supreme Court. Curt Gentry described him as 'a hypochondriac who became a national hero, a bachelor obsessed with sexual slander. J Edgar Hoover literally changed the course of US history with files known in the Justice Department as 'twelve drawers full of political cancer"'. These files, and their skilful use, helped him imperil the liberties of the American people, and to subvert the constitution as he siphoned power unto himself.

There may be much argument about whether Hoover used—or sought to use—his power for the public good, in spite of the demands of democracy and its flawed institutions. In a sense this would place him in the same mould as Fouché, Himmler and Beria, who in their own way were also able to convince themselves that they too were patriots.

Perhaps Samuel Johnson was right when Boswell recorded him saying 'Patriotism is the last refuge of a scoundrel'.

At 77 years of age, Hoover remained the unsackable Director of the FBI. On Tuesday 2 May 1972, he was expected in his office but he lay collapsed and dead sprawled on the floor in his house. He was to be given the highest accolade of state approbation by lying in state, followed by a state funeral, and an oration by the then President, Richard Nixon. Of course, in many ways, Hoover differs from other high police in that the use and extent of his powers were never to result in such human degradation and suffering as earlier described, but it is in the acquisition of power and its cunning and unconstitutional deployment where comparisons can be made.

When set against the criteria of principled policing, democratic models, as might be expected, fair best. But even here, as in Hoover's case, there is ample scope for gross abuse of power.

SUMMARY: SETTING GOALS AND STANDARDS

To what extent can the discussion in this chapter assist when setting principles, standards and goals for a police organization?

In our brush with utilitarianism, it failed to recommend itself as a guiding theory, due largely to moral ethical uncertainties, although police service can contribute to aspects of the doctrine.

Through Karl Popper we have acquired the theory of protectionism based on his assessment of Lychophron's ideas: the law is 'a covenant by which men assure one another of justice' and the state 'a co-operative association for the prevention of crime'. Popper also posed a prerequisite for police leaders: 'Only if he knows what he wants can he decide whether [his institution] is or is not well adapted to its function'. He further demands 'protection' for his own freedom [individualism] and for 'other people's freedoms [altruism]'. The freedom which is to be protected is that which 'does not harm other citizens'; and all this is to be characterised by 'the qualities of equalitarianism, individualism, and protectionism against injustice'.

In considering the theory of the social contract (which in its particular form Popper claims the primacy for Lychophron), we accepted the criticism of the historicist theory of Hume and others. On the other hand, Russell tells us that the theory has some measure of truth 'as legal fiction to justify government'.

Justice as fairness, raised by John Rawls, is of prime concern to the high police if they are to understand many of the politics surrounding their place in the order of things. Kant's explanation of just coercion, reinforced by Popper's comments, is of central importance, as is the Rule of Law especially when it is endowed by constitutional and moral rectitude.

Police aims and expectations: the 'common good'

So—before embarking on *Chapter 2*—it might be said that the primary and guiding political principles of policing should be concerned with, and directed towards the theory of the common good of society.[53] The aim of policing is not to enforce the law and coerce the people for its own sake, but to do so for the common good, and that is a good which places freedom above all other political values (duties are important but they arise only out of freedom). As Kant insists, there can be no sacrifice of the dignity of people for the benefit of others, even though the others are powerful and influential, since if this were to be the case there is no good which is common, and the principle of equalitiarianism would have been denied. When we speak of 'keeping the peace'—which is a joint and ancient responsibility of government and people at common law (an express contract)—we have the common good in mind, since the peace facilitates freedom for all.

Police may also be expected to protect the common good against the actions of the more powerful, or numerous. An example might be where the common good requires that every person who wishes to go to a place of employment should have the right to do so, whilst during a trade dispute others seek to stop them. It is in the common good, even for *pro tem* pickets themselves, that the right to go to work be upheld.

It may also be said that freedom of speech and assembly are 'common goods', and should be protected, even, or especially, where the purpose is for protest, be it vehement and controversial. Thus what are called 'extremists' have a right to hold their views and to express them, though this is subject to limitations for the common good.

The point at which a narrow common good becomes harmful to the wider common good of society, e.g. in the form of provocation of disorder and violence, calls for a nice sense of judgment, but police are required to have this and to act. Man is essentially a social animal and some notion of common good is an imperative both for happy survival, and of civilisation. Since, by its nature, the common good is to protect individual rights there is no conflict between the concept and the plural society.

The police function might best be understood, and articulated through the philosophical theory of the social contract, even conceding that neither it, nor other theories of government, are likely to offer the perfect answer. At the end of the day, as Clausewitz reminds us, in the practical arts, it is 'experience which is their proper soil'.

43

Three elements identified

Finally it is possible to synthesise the three elements which appear to support the theory of principled policing. These are:

- *social contract theory* as advanced in Rawl's conception of 'justice as fairness'. Although the theory of the social contract as an abstract idea might thus be seen as remaining unchangeable, its terms or contents cannot do so. They must change as societies change. The terms of the social contract in the former USSR were markedly different from those which now exist in the new liberal democracies which have emerged from the Soviet bloc. Amongst the most important of these changes are principles of policing, particularly in relation to freedom, and the remit and powers of the former secret police. Further strengthening of the contractarian society is likely to emerge from the growing characteristics of civil society.

   Even in liberal democracies, in recent time, many adjustments to the terms of the social contract have had to be made to ensure that justice keeps pace with plural and multi-racial characteristics. For example policing principles have been required to adjust to protect minorities from discrimination, and to protect the legitimate expectations of justice for women. It is important—with more change ahead—to be constantly laying claim to co-operation between, and the morality of, both people and government. Constant attention to the ideals of the theoretical contract is also a test for the efficacy of developing policing from principles.

   Not only do the terms of the contract change, but the frontiers also. There is a constant process of expansion to bring within its moral compass the alienated, and the 'Barbarians'. There is now a contract to deal with the whole human family within the terms of the Universal Declaration of Human Rights, and e.g. to prosecute war criminals through an international social contract theory.

   The role of the police in its widest moral sense can be conceived as advancing and facilitating contractarian purposes, not in a purely theoretical way as legislators, but in a practical way within the actual life of society day by day. Police have to expect not simply to be called upon to exercise force, but to acquire an understanding of how to deal with people constructively in their role as trustees of the social contract, establishing cooperation and morality based on justice as fairness.

- the *theory of protectionism* as promulgated by Popper. Protection of contractarian freedoms would rest on the theory of protectionism as described by Popper, the principles of which are

44

equalitarianism, individualism, and protectionism from injustice which must be central to the morality of principled policing; and

• the *theory of policing the common good* as discussed in detail under the previous heading.

The police as trustees
Finally, the police function should be based on the notion and principle of trusteeship. Trusteeship carries with it moral obligations such as those of honourable and ethical conduct in the application of power and authority. As trustees under the social contract police are required to use their position 'constructively', and that is what the remainder of this book seeks to examine.

Endnotes

1. Scarman Report, *The Brixton Disorders 10-12 April 1981*, Cmnd. 8427, London: HMSO
2. *Times Literary Supplement*, 23 June, 1995
3. *Today* newspaper, 20 May, pp. 4-5
4. Browning, Christopher K, *Ordinary Men*, Harper Collins :New York, 1992
5. Ibid., p. 73
6. (1884), 14 QBD 273
7. Hudson, W D, *A Century of Moral Philosophy*, Lutterworth Press: London, 1980
8. Ibid., *Modern Moral Philosophy*, 2nd Ed., Macmillan: London, 1983, p. 384
9. *Oxford Dictionary of Philosophy*, Oxford University Press, 1994
10. Ibid., p. 388
11. Hudson, op. cit, p. 398
12. Hare, R M *Moral Thinking*, Oxford University Press, 1981, p. 2 et. seq.
13. Hudson, op. cit, p. 426
14. Seanor and Fotion, *Hare and Critics*, Oxford University Press, 1988
15. *Cameron Report: Disturbances in Northern Ireland*, Cmnd. 532, London: HMSO
16. Kant, Immanuel, *The Metaphysical Elements of Justice*, Bobbs-Merrill: New York, 1965, p. ix
17. Russell, B, *History of Western Philosophy*, Unwin: London, 1961, p. 742
18. Bullock, Alan, *Hitler: A Study in Tyranny*, Penguin: London, 1963, pp. 262-3
19. Williams, Bernard, *Morality: An Introduction to Ethics*, Cambridge University Press, 1972, p. 112
20. Sabine, George H, *A History of Political Theory*, Harrap: London, 1971, p. 673
21. Rawls, John, *A Theory of Justice*, Oxford University Press, 1973, p. 573
22. Popper, Karl R, *The Open Society and Its Enemies*, Routledge: London, 1989, pp. 114-117
23. Ibid., p. 109-110
24. Ibid., p. 119
25. Russell, op. cit., p. 610
26. Royal Institute of International Affairs, *International Affairs*, Vol. 72, No. 2, April 1995, p. 259
27. Maine, Sir Henry, *Ancient Law*, Dent: London, 1917
28. Ibid., p. 100
29. Popper, op. cit., p. 115
30. Kant, op. cit., p. 33

31. Rawls, op. cit.
32. Rawls, op. cit., p. 3 et seq.
33. Ibid., pp. 302-303
34. 3 WLR 961
35. Rawls, op. cit., pp. 314-315
36. Kant, op. cit., pp. 35-36
37. Dicey, A V, *An Introduction to the Law of the Constitution*, 10th Ed., Macmillan: London, 1997, p. 187 et seq
38. Fuller, L L, *The Morality of Law* (Revised Edition)
39. Stead, P J, *Pioneers in Policing*, MacGraw-Hill: Maidenhead, 1977, p. 72
40. Chapman, B, *Police State*, Pall Mall: London, 1970, p. 29
41. Ibid., p. 30
42. Gash, N, *Peel*, Longman: London, 1976, p. 104 et. seq.
43. Knight, Amy, *Stalin's First Lieutenant*, Princeton University: Princeton, USA, 1993
44. Sakharov, Andrei, *Memoirs*, Hutchinson: London, 1990
45. Khrushchev, Nikita, *Khrushchev Remembers*, Deutsch: London, 1971
46. Padfield, Peter, *Himmler*, Macmillan: London, 1990
47. Hohne, Heinz, *The Order of the Death's Head*, Pan: London, 1972
48. Ibid., pp. 46-69
49. Padfield, op. cit., p. 596
50. Gentry, Curt, *J. Edgar Hoover*, Norton: New York, 1991
51. Ibid., p. 62
52. Ibid.
53. Alderson, John, *Policing Freedom*, Macdonald and Evans, 1979, pp. 166-7.

CHAPTER 2

The People's Peace

Amongst the fruits to be expected from the contractarian society, as we have chosen to describe it, would be a tolerable state of *peace* and *order*. How then are we to account for public *disorder* which is so central to the existence, purpose, and function of police?

MORAL FAILURE

It is my view that public disobedience on a significant scale is an indication of moral fault somewhere, and even though it may sometimes be inevitable, it remains an indication of such failure. In a liberal democracy where the means exist to bring about political change through constitutional channels, public disobedience is also an indication of political failure. In repressive or malfunctioning regimes, disobedience, even revolt, may always be anticipated—and this is one reason why such regimes require more powerful police than their democratic counterparts.

Where political dissent is unknown, or is not allowed, the policing of dissent, its nature and limits, will not be understood. In such cases police action is likely to contravene international morality as contained in the Universal Declaration of Human Rights.

I have always believed that policing should not aim for a state of order which is too strict and contrived, but one which might better be described as 'orderly disorder'. Policing should seek to help produce a climate in which the politics of creative disorder may have a part to play. In a sense the policing of people *en masse* requires the capacity to give gently, as a tree may bend with the wind—but to hold firm when it is vital to do so.

In a liberal democracy the outcome is to be seen at its best where police and people have an instinct about protest, in which both sides desire to win, and have an ability to contrive this outcome. It happened famously in London's Grosvenor Square, site of the USA Embassy, on 27 October 1968. There had been many violent confrontations between young political protesters and police at this time in major cities in different parts of the world, concerning anti-Vietnam War protest and other moral issues, and there was apprehension that the same violence was about to happen in London.

A crowd—estimated at more than 30,000 people—marched through London escorted by ordinary police (there were no riot or armed police in England at the time) to the Embassy, which was protected by a police cordon. Throughout the day and evening the protest was conducted with virtually no violence. (In the event the British gave a striking display of civilised behaviour).

The home secretary at the time, James Callaghan, spoke to the world's press in Grosvenor Square after the protesters had dispersed, praising both people and police for their restraint, and not surprisingly he thought that the conduct on both sides was a unique example of civic behaviour. The chief London correspondent of the *Washington Post* writing in *The Times* praised the event as 'a moral example':

> What did not happen, quite simply, was something that has occurred in every other major western country this year, a truly violent confrontation between angry students and sadistic police.[2]

I am of the opinion that in this case both the public and the police owed much to a cultural tradition, and a propensity for regarding the keeping of the peace as a mutual obligation.

THE PEOPLE'S PEACE EXAMINED

Let us then enquire further into this concept of what I will call 'The People's Peace', since I believe that it exemplifies a maturing of social contractual tradition between people and government and as between people themselves. A former British Home Office permanent under secretary of state described it as

> . . . the maintenance of conditions under which the normal functions of government can be carried on, where obedience to the law is adequately secured, and the people are free to pursue their lawful ends without threat of interference.[3]

Traditions in this regard differ. Maine describes the centralising tendencies of Imperial Rome:

> The theory of criminal justice had in fact worked round almost to the point where it started. It had begun in the belief that it was the business of the collective community to avenge its own wrongs by its own hand; and it ended in an especial manner to the Sovereign as representative and mandatory of his people.[4]

The English system on the other hand developed *locally* and in large part remains local to this day. In medieval England,

> ... the primary importance of the vills in governmental life lay in the police duties which came to be imposed upon them ... the system relied upon the principle that all members of a community accepted an obligation for the good behaviour of each other.[5]

This comment represents a strong endorsement of social contract theory, and as recently as 1929 a Royal Commission on the police in England commented:

> ... the police of this country have never been recognised either in law or by tradition as a force distinct from the general body of citizens.[6]

In France on the other hand, according to Stead, the early police of the marshalls of France, the *Marechausse*, were a paid body which

> ... had policed the highways and rural areas of the country since the end of the Middle Ages, incarnating the Royal Authority throughout the land.[7]

There is much more of Rome in the character of the French system than in that of the Anglo-Saxon which is more heir to early Germanic traditions.

> From early times, certainly from the reign of King Alfred (871-900) the primary responsibility for maintaining the King's Peace fell upon each locality under a well understood principle of social obligation or collective.[8]

Even following the Norman Conquest (1066) little changed in this regard apart from a decided strengthening of the system. A further and perhaps more ancient example of this police business was brought to my notice by a friend who was Inspector General of Police in the Punjab in the difficult 1980s and who later became vice-chancellor of the University of Bhopal. He wrote:

> I discovered that throughout its history, the Indian Police has been a ruler friendly agency, and not a citizen's police. It was so during the British Colonial governance. What is remarkable is that it continues to be so even after Independence. That's why, unlike your police [the British] the Indian Police has never had a pleasant relationship with the Indian people. It has served and continues to serve, the establishment, the affluent, and the powerful.[9]

It is neither possible nor is it desirable at this stage to go further into the historical detail of police systems, interesting though it may be. I hope that the foregoing brief comments will have led to the view that the principles of the theory of the people's peace are not incompatible with the social contract theory of government. We now have to consider the problem for principled policing when it is confronted by political dissent, particularly when we pause to reflect that dissent in the past has at times resulted in important progress of mankind.

At a more trivial level, I used to remind my police officers how much they owed for improvements in their professional status and conditions of service to their forbears who went on strike in 1918 in defiance of the regulations governing their behaviour.[10] The police strikers were dismissed, but their colleagues' position was enhanced. A crisis in policing was brought about in Victoria, Australia, in 1923, and with similar results.[11]

CIVIL DISOBEDIENCE AND PRINCIPLED POLICING

The subject of civil disobedience confronts principled policing with its greatest challenge. On the face of it there can be no doubt where the police duty lies, and this is well summed up in the words of the former solicitor-general of the United States, and Dean of Harvard Law School, Erwin Griswold, quoted by Dworkin. [12]

[It] is the essence of the law, that it is equally applied to all, that it binds all alike, irrespective of personal motive. For this reason one who contemplates disobedience out of moral conviction should not be surprised, and must not be bitter if a criminal conviction ensues. And he must accept the fact that organized society cannot endure on any other basis.

This statement is of interest for at least two reasons: the first of these is that it would seem to most decent police officers to be a correct summary; and the second is that it just as easily might be said of the Constitution of the former USSR. In both cases in practice, the strict letter of the Constitution may be modified through necessary interpretation. During the protests against being drafted into the US army to fight in Vietnam, it was argued, amongst other things, that the war was constitutionally illegal, since '. . . the President has exercised war-making power without the Declaration of Congress as required in article 1, section 8 of the US Constitution'.[13] If true this would have justified the civil disobedience of the conscientious objectors. The law by no means seemed to be clear.

Dissidence in the former Soviet Union was, relatively, an equally hazardous business, although the Constitution guaranteed freedom of speech, of assembly, of meetings, street processions, and demonstrations (article 50 (1977)), and as in the USA, all 'Citizens of the USSR are equal before the law (article 34 (1977))'. Consider the following example: the US dissidents against the war in Vietnam were no doubt moved by the same humanity as their Soviet counterparts, but when it comes to punishment for breaking the law—as Dworkin points out,[15] and as every experienced police officer knows—the prosecuting authorities in the USA, as in the UK, have wide discretion to prosecute or not to prosecute in criminal cases. It is equally true that in cases of mass civil disobedience most of the dissenters are not, and cannot be arrested or proceeded against. To consider prosecuting a token few is always less than satisfactory, but even more so where the law is doubtful and the motive is beneficient towards society; such circumstances provide ample scope for decisions not to prosecute non-violent dissent without undermining the Rule of Law. After all we are concerned here with the good of the people, most of whom either understand these issues, or who are receptive towards an understanding of them.

It is of interest to note that the British Campaign for Nuclear Disarmament in 1960 organized a 'Committee of 100' in order to confound the police authorities. One hundred people signed a statement declaring their willingness to break the law in protest against the British government's possession of nuclear weapons. The offences anyone would commit would be obstruction, or trespass of military bases. The strategy was that when members of the committee were arrested others would be available to take their place. The result was that there would always be leaders.

What then are we to do to provide principled policing of social and political dissidence? When the upholders of order and the enforcers of laws, the police, are trustees of the social contract, it seems to be a contradiction that this coercive arm of government should be required to be pusillanimous. Can a contract to abide by majority rule allow a minority to disrupt the social order which is the very product of the same contract? Perhaps we should have recourse once again to the words of John Locke:

> Great mistakes in the ruling part, many wrong and inconvenient laws, and all the slips of human frailty will be borne by the people without mutiny or murmur.[17]

51

MARTIN LUTHER KING

It is only when injustices become unbearable, either for the protesters themselves, or for those whose moral conscience rebels on behalf of justice, that protest and dissent can be expected. This undoubtedly was the case with the Civil Rights Movement in the US led by Martin Luther King, whose moral courage, and charismatic leadership, were quite remarkable. His 'Letter from Birmingham City Jail'[18] published in the year before the USA became embroiled in the Vietnam war is a classic of its kind. His letter is replete with compelling justification for civil disobedience towards the segregationist laws of some of the southern states of America, and the general denial of the political and social rights of black people. Consider the following passages:

> Birmingham is probably the most segregated city in the United States. Its ugly record of police brutality is known in every section of this country. Its unjust treatment of Negroes in the courts is a notorious reality. There have been more unsolved bombings of Negro homes and churches in Birmingham than in any other city in this nation. These are the hard brutal facts. On the basis of these conditions Negro leaders sought to negotiate with the city fathers. But the political leaders consistently refused to engage in good faith negotiation.

and

> But when you have seen vicious mobs lynch your mothers and fathers at will, and drown your sisters and brothers at whim; when you have seen hate-filled policemen curse, kick, brutalise, and even kill your black brothers and sisters with impunity etc., etc.

and

> An unjust law is a code inflicted upon a minority which that minority had no part in enacting or creating because they did not have the unhampered right to vote . . . there are some counties without a single Negro registered to vote despite the fact that the Negro constitutes a majority of the population.

Martin Luther King was arrested for deliberately parading in Birmingham without a permit. He and his fellow protesters were thus arrested for doing what the First Amendment to the US Constitution provides for, i.e. peaceful assembly and peaceful protest. He believed that there is nothing wrong with a an ordinance which requires a permit for a parade, but when it is used to preserve segregation and to deny constitutional rights it becomes unjust. In his letter, King sets out what he as an activist, and not a theorist, considers to be the four basic steps in a non-violent campaign:

1. Collection of facts to determine whether injustices are alive.
2. Negotiation.
3. Self purification; and
4. Direct action.

DEFINING CIVIL DISOBEDIENCE

The philosopher's definition of civil disobedience which Rawls adopts from Bedau[19] is 'a public, non-violent political act contrary to law, usually done with the aim of bringing about a change in the law, or policies of government. The law, or the policy, being objected to need not be directly breached'. Even though this definition may be regarded as narrow, it certainly is wide enough to accommodate Martin Luther King's campaign principles.

It is timely to examine some of the philosophical contributions to the literature on civil disobedience generated by two decades of political protest and public disorder in the US, i.e. 1955 to 1975. Since we have adopted John Rawl's contractarian society as our paradigm, I will first of all turn to his theory on the subject of civil disobedience.

With Rawls we start form the position of a legitimately established democratic authority in which 'the role and appropriateness of civil disobedience' to that authority by citizens 'who recognise and accept the legitimacy of the constitution' is considered. We are not considering resistance to a tyrannical system in which John Locke's theory of the justification of the use of violence with which to overthrow such system would be more appropriate.

Rawls[20] puts the question: 'At what point does the duty to comply with laws enacted by a legislative majority (or with executive acts supported by that majority, e.g. police action) cease to be binding in view of the right to defend one's liberties and the duty to oppose injustice'.

Following this theory is crucial for police, since it questions the limits of democratic government and majority rule, and also involves consideration of the moral basis of democracy, as Rawls points out, and thereby the morality of the policing of civil disobedience. It raises what might be called the 'tyranny of the majority'—which we noted to be a problem in the southern states of the US, and we shall see it again in Northern Ireland when we come to consider events there in due course.

Rawls insists that his theory of civil disobedience is 'designed only for the special case of a nearly just society'. He does not claim too much for it; he merely advances it to give definition to a perspective within which he can approach the problem and to give weight to relevant considerations. It 'seeks to clear the vision, and make judgments about it more coherent'.

A 'very nearly just society' by its very definition would have to find a place for protest and dissent which aim to oppose injustice, for to allow otherwise would contradict that definition. To outlaw civil disobedience in every form would be to endanger rather than to protect democracy. The incapacity to be disobedient must take some of the blame when democracy is hijacked as in Italy and Germany during the 1920s and 1930s:

> Hitler never abandoned the cloak of legality; he recognised the enormous psychological value of having the law on his side.[21]

Those who might have said 'No' to Hitler, were either outwitted as Alan Bullock says, and, 'like the young lady of Riga who smiled as she rode on a tiger', swallowed—or were attracted by his extreme brand of nationalism. The few brave souls who tried to say 'No' were eliminated. He turned the law inside out, 'making illegality legal'.

In their Fascist regimes both Hitler and Mussolini, from the beginning, *took over the policing systems of their country at the very first opportunity*, precluding any prospect of principled policing. During the Nuremberg trials[22] of Nazi war criminals and in the trial of Adolph Eichmann in Jerusalem, the defence of 'obedience to orders' where this involved crimes against humanity was not acceptable. The United Nations Code of Conduct for Law Enforcement Officials provides for the right to disobey unlawful orders.[23] Eric Fromm has trenchant views on this issue:

> A person can become free through acts of disobedience by learning to say "No" to power. But not only is the capacity for disobedience the condition for freedom, freedom is also the condition for disobedience. If I am afraid of freedom, I cannot dare to say "No", I cannot have the courage to be disobedient . . . Indeed freedom and the capacity for disobedience are inseparable; *hence any social, political, and religious system which proclaims freedom, yet stamps out disobedience, cannot speak the truth.*[24] (emphasis supplied)

Fromm's words cut through the arguments like a surgeon's knife.

Justice indivisible
Justice in its true form is indivisible and is not always on the side of the law, therefore to obey the law is not always to obey justice. Justice is

always moral (for the difficulty in defining justice see the earlier reference to Kant (p. 33)). It may be moral *at times* to defy the law, but to defy justice *never.*

Endnotes

1. Critchley, T A, *The Conquest of Violence*, Constable: London, 1970, p. 1
2. Ibid.
3. Newsome, Sir Frank, *The Home Office*, 1954
4. Maine, Sir Richard, *Ancient Law, Everyman*: London, 1914
5. Sayles, G O, *The Medieval Foundations of England*, London, 1948, p. 188
6. *Royal Commission on Police Powers and Procedure*, London: HMSO, 1929, Cmnd. 3297
7. Stead, P J, *Pioneers in Policing*, McGraw and Hill: Maidenhead, 1977, p. 5
8. Critchley, T A, *A History of Police in England and Wales*, Constable: London, 1978 (Revised Edition), p. 2
9. Personal letter to the author, 1995
10. Critchley, op. cit., p. 185
11. O'Brien, G M, *The Australian Police Forces*, Oxford University Press: London, 1960, pp. 64-66
12. Dworkin, R, *Taking Rights Seriously*, Duckworth: London, 1977, p. 208
13. Finer, S E, *Five Constitutions*, London, 1979, p. 95
14. Sakharov, Andrei, Memoirs, Hutchinson: London, 1990, p. 331
15. Dworkin, op. cit., p. 217
16. Ryan, Alan, *Bertrand Russell*, Allen Lane: London, 1988, p. 193
17. Locke, John, *The Second Treatise on Civil Government*, Prometheus; New York, 1986, p. 121
18. Bedau, H A, *Civil Disobedience*, Pegasus: New York, 1969, p. 62
19. Rawls, John, *A Theory of Justice*, Oxford University Press, 1973, p. 364
20. Ibid., p. 363
21. Bullock, Alan, *Hitler: A Study in Tyranny*, Pelican: London, 1962, pp. 255-7
22. Tusa, Ann and John, *The Nuremberg Trial*, Macmillan: London, 1983, p. 87
23. United Nations Code for Law Enforcement Officials, article 3
24. Fromm, Eric, *On Disobedience*, Seabury Press: New York, 1981, p. 21.

CHAPTER 3

The Police Ethos and the Doctrine of Human Rights

At the time of writing evidence is all around us of human failure to govern policing so as to serve democracy in its highest form, and ignorance of what might be called the Human Rights mission of police is widespread within the world's police systems with very few exceptions.

Since the promulgation of the Universal Declaration of Human Rights in 1948, and its progeny, in particular the European Convention of Human Rights and Fundamental Freedoms of 1950, the European Commission and European Court, police practice in both national and international contexts has been challenged to aspire to legal and moral dimensions worthy of the ideals set out in the preamble to the UN Declaration. These include, 'recognition of the inherent dignity and of the equal and inalienable rights of all mankind as the foundation of freedom, justice and peace in the world'.[1] Before examining the *status quo* of police and human rights, I would like to take up two or three of the more contentious views of the police ethos.

PART I: THE POLICE ETHOS

It is said that the professional police ethos is 'an amoral one, as proven by the constantly observed phenomenon that professional policemen make the transition from one regime to another without difficulty',[2] and that 'their professional ethic discounts the ideological nature of the regime they are serving'.[3] It is further alleged that

> . . . the arbitrary use of police powers, brutality, spying, secrecy, the temptation to act as a law unto itself are characteristics inherent in every police system. *They stem from the very nature of police work.*[4] (Emphasis supplied)

I now want to test these assertions and to do so I propose to use the German experience. However, before we embark on an examination of the police ethos, it must be stressed that these matters are fundamentally influenced and determined by the culture and politics of societies themselves. The police being the coercive arm of the state are custodians of a battery of powers, and of force, which lend themselves to abuse. I once summed up this phenomenon as follows:

> The police, like laws, reflect the nature of the society which they serve: corrupt societies . . . get corrupt police, totalitarian societies acquire omnipotent police, tolerant societies have tolerant police, wise societies bridle police powers.[5]

The German case: or 'Hitler's Enforcers'[6]

What commends the German National Socialist (Nazi) period of government (1933-45) for examination in this present context is that, unlike the Soviet Union, it was born out of a democracy, the Weimar Republic, and not out of a revolution. As Bullock points out in his study of Hitler, he was most determined that his political ambition to govern Germany should '. . . never abandon[ed] the cloak of legality. He recognised the enormous psychological value of having the law on his side'.[7] Hitler's subsequent seizure of dictatorial powers of government, and rule by decree, are now common knowledge and well documented.

Speaking at a symposium in Frankfurt on Main in May 1995, Professor Joseph Nolte, leader of the European Centre at Tubingen University, reminded his audience of police officers and others that

> People often forget that the so-called Gestapo (Secret State Police) mainly consisted of police officers who had already started their careers during the Empire, or during the Republic of Weimar.[8]

In other words they were just ordinary professional police officers.

Arthur Nebe was a senior German (Prussian) police official in the robberies division of the pre-Nazi Berlin Police. A Nazi supporter since 1931 whilst a serving police officer, later executive head of the Gestapo (administration) and subsequently head of Kripo (Criminal Police), Nebe believed that 'there are no such things as principles only circumstances',[9] which is an excellent example of the amoral dimension of the police ethos, and the antithesis of one of the purposes of this book. In pursuit of his blatant opportunism he became sponsoring member of the SS, joined the SA (Nazi Stormtroopers) and was leader of many like-minded professional police officers.

Nebe and his cronies were of considerable influence in helping the plotting and scheming SS Reichsfuhrer, Heinrich Himmler to bring the entire German police machine under Himmler's, and therefore under Hitler's, total control. The headquarters of the Gestapo in Berlin was used as an illegal detention centre where torture and brutality were notorious.[10] Nebe was later described by SS Chief Kalternbrunner as 'a two faced character with an unhealthy degree of ambition . . . Nebe would ruthlessly push aside anything which stood in his path to promotion'. His subsequent scheming whilst head of Himmler's Kripo led in 1944 to his execution for being involved in a conspiracy to bring about the downfall of Hitler.[11]

Another centre of police perfidy was to be found in the Bavarian, Munich Police headquarters where the professional police officers included another ambitious and amoral senior police official, Heinrich Muller, later known as Gestapo Muller, who was just one of a majority of professional police officers willing to follow the Nazi path. During the Weimar Republic, Muller had been in charge of the anti-Communist desk in the political section of the Munich police headquarters. He was apparently 'detested' by the Upper Bavarian Nazi Party Gau as a police officer '. . . who at times would disregard rules and regulations' and who was 'a violent opponent of Communism'. Muller it is said, 'would have acted similarly against the right wing. *Being incredibly ambitious . . . he would be bent on recognition from his superiors under any system'.*[12] (emphasis supplied) This archetypal amoral police officer and his kind are well represented in the ranks of most police organizations. Muller's cunning self-serving professionalism led to his appointment as head of the Gestapo and with it the responsibility for atrocious extremes of inhuman barbarity. No extreme of inhumanity ordered by Himmler was too great for Muller's amoral professionalism, as he despatched the legions of the doomed to the Nazi concentration camps. Muller was the typical

> middle-rank official; of limited imagination, non-political, non-ideological, his only fanaticism lay in an inner drive to perfection in his profession and in his duties to the state, which in his mind were one. That the state happened to be Hitler's Third Reich was a matter of circumstance . . .[13]

'Enemies of the people'
In his speech in the Reichstag on 20 Febraury 1938, Hitler defined enemies of the people in the following terms:

> Above all a man who feels it is his duty at such an hour to assume the leadership of his people is not responsible to the laws of Parliamentary usage or to a particular democratic conception, but solely to the mission placed upon him. *And anyone who interfered with this mission is an enemy of the people.*[14] (Emphasis supplied)

Urged on by this warped viewpoint, the police were soon busy rounding up and incarcerating the so-called 'enemies of the people' to the point where the gaols were overflowing. The enterprising Munich SS opened a concentration camp at Dachau into which those opposing Hitler's will, such as Social Democrats, Communists, Bavarian People's Party members, Jewish businessmen, and journalists opposing the Nazi regime were imprisoned. It was deemed 'impossible to allow these officials their freedom again'.[15]

Amalgamation: A crucial decision
In 1936, by decree, Hitler appointed Himmler Chief of all the German police who were to be gradually embraced by Himmler's SS. Himmler, 'amalgamated the criminal detection and Gestapo positions throughout the Reich into a Sicherheitspolizei [Security Police] and the urban uniformed police into a single Ordnungspolizei [literally, 'order-keeping police].'[16]

Owing to his knowledge of the Soviet police system, Bavarian police officer Heinrich Muller was now appointed to the top position in the Berlin Gestapo office. As head of the Gestapo throughout the Reich, and its conquered territories, Muller became the most powerful professional police officer of all. (After the war he just 'disappeared'). The most 'ruthless, most unprincipled people' from the Ordnungspolizei were selected to be members of the Nazi Party's internal intelligence service, the notorious SD of the SS.[17]

Oath-taking
Oaths are a common enough phenomenon in political systems from the primitive to the advanced. They are a device which is intended to secure the loyalty of state officials to their constitutional, or contractual role. They are not matters to be taken lightly, since solemn oaths rest on the consciences of those who take or accept them, particularly those oaths which are sworn on a powerful deity, such as God.

On a visit to the former colony of Sierra Leone I recall being approached by an African assistant commissioner of police who was agitated as he wished to divest himself of the burden of the oath which he had taken to serve the British Queen in colonial times. 'Was there a formula?', he asked, which would release him from those obligations. I have also heard German soldiers declare that having sworn to serve the Fuhrer they felt honour bound to do whatever he required of them. There seemed to be no question of whether their actions were legal, moral or humane.

German police oaths: 1933 and 1934
On becoming Reich Chancellor on 30 January 1933, Hitler decreed that the oath of office required under the Weimar Republic be abolished, and

a new oath of allegiance was introduced. On 2 December 1933, President von Hindenburg signed Decree No. 136 which enacted oaths of allegiance as follows:

1. *Civil servants (includes police)* I swear I will keep faith with People and the Fatherland; keep the Constitution and the Decrees, and fulfil my duties conscientiously, so help me God.

The invocation of God seeks to give the oath a divine quality, and one which rests heavily on the individual's conscience.

2 *Soldiers of the military* I swear by Almighty God this Holy Oath; I will always serve my People and the Fatherland faithfully and obediently, and as a courageous soldier at any time be ready to give my life for this Oath.

This oath not only rests heavily on the individual's conscience but as would be expected it demands the ultimate sacrifice.

Heraclitis, the Greek philosopher (c500 BC), is quoted by Karl Popper in *The Open Society and It's Enemies* as saying that 'The law can demand too that the will of one man be obeyed'. Shortly after the above decree was implemented, President Hindenberg died, and Adolph Hitler became head of state; now the oaths could be re-cast and, decisively, they were. Decree No. 98 of 22 August 1934 called for the administering of fresh forms of oaths as follows:

1. *Civil servants* I swear I will be true and obedient to Adolph Hitler, Leader of the German Reich and People, be true to the laws and fulfil my duties diligently, so help me God.

2 *Soldiers of military* [includes SS and Gestapo] I swear by God this Holy Oath, I will give total obedience to Adolph Hitler, Leader of the German Reich and People, the Supreme Commander of the military, and as a courageous soldier prepared to lay down my life at any time.

By this same decree Hitler delegated the power of appointment to the most important government posts to his top officials, retaining the right to intervene in 'special cases'. It was no doubt under this provision that SS Reichsfuhrer Himmler was able to exert his powerful influence over the police and indeed over the Holocaust.

Henceforth the implied social contract between police and the people was to be one *between police and dictator*, a position which John Locke might have said justified rebellion.

Codes

Codes are comprised of rules and regulations which seek to modify and control the conduct of those to whom they apply. Codes sometimes carry punitive sanctions for failure to comply with their provisions, and these would include police discipline codes where they exist. The Police Discipline Code in Great Britain, e.g. creates 16 offences ranging from 'discreditable conduct' to 'criminal conduct' in cases where a police officer has been convicted of a criminal offence by a court of law. Punishments range from admonition to dismissal.

The United Nation's Code of Conduct for Law Enforcement Officials on the other hand can exact no punishment since there is no mandated provision for such measures. Other professions use codes of ethics which seek to raise the ethical standards of their members; the most famous perhaps being the Hippocractic Oath which remains central to codes of medical ethics in many countries (Hippocrates: Fifth century BC).

The German police code 1935

In 1935, Hitler's Minister of Home Affairs, Wilhelm Frick, published a code of ethics for the German police as follows:

Basic principles for the police (1935)

i   Keep your oath faithfully and with total dedication t o the Fuhrer and the People and your Country.

ii   The exceptional rights which you have been granted as visible representative of state power are not privileges but obligations. Be an example as a servant of your people.

iii   Be attentive and keep quiet in police matters, be brave and self-confident, but be just and unscrupulous when struggling against all enemies of the people and state.

iv   Treat others like you would like to be treated in their place.

v   Be honest, modest and simple. Lies are mean; presents oblige you; thirst for pleasure is undignified.

vi   Help those who need your help.

vii   Do not neglect your outward appearance it mirrors your inward appearance.

viii   Be obedient to your superiors. Be an example for your subordinates. Keep sexual self-control [then called 'Manneszucht'] and cultivate comradeship.

    ix   Carrying a weapon makes you participate in the biggest honour of a German man, always keep this in mind. [A classic example of the military ethos].

    x   Educate yourself and keep educating. Those who achieve much are acknowledged. Acknowledgements are your highest prize.

These then were the directives which were to be at the service of Hitler and his Nazi government.

Professor Pastor Dr. Dieter Beese, lecturer in professional ethics at Germany's Police Leadership Academy at Hiltrup, Munster, asks 'Is the profession of a police officer connected with a special moral demand?' He points out that the history of the German ethos of public service illustrates that German officials always attached great importance to some traditional values such as, faithfulness, punctuality, conscientiousness, loyalty, industry, obedience, devotion, and moderation. But he believes that this ethos of public service is a problem in itself since it is a legacy of a pre-democratic ethos which carries with it 'some historical burdens'.

Military influence

In nineteenth century Prussia the political atmosphere was dominated by the values of the military (and of course most of the police had served in the military). Dieter Beese is of the view that officials in the Weimar Republic 'lived in opposition to their own democratic constitution', by which he no doubt means that though the form of government was designed to be democratic the substance was authoritarian and autocratic.

In his account of European police forces before 1914, Raymond Fosdick, Commissioner of Accounts for the City of New York, records the military nature of the German police officers who came directly from the *unteroffizier* ranks (i.e. they were non-commissioned officers) with at least nine years' military service—'we prefer a longer service in the army if we can secure it', was the view of Hamburg's police president. Fosdick recorded his surprise at the lack of democratic control of police which was just 'a huge bureaucratic machine' involving 'the great powers of the police official, his right to fine and imprison without judicial process, his exemption from prosecution for false arrest which breeds an arrogance hardly to be tolerated in democratic countries'.[19]

Fosdick's views were given credence by the comments of Thomas Mann, German writer of the time, who links German militarism with German spiritual and moral characteristics:

Our soldierliness has an intimate spiritual connection with our moralism; indeed while other cultures have a tendency to assume civilian forms of cultural behaviour into the most refined aspects of life, into art, German militarism is in truth the form and revelation of German morality.[19]

Thus it was that the German police during the Nazi period were heirs to some powerful military, i.e. war-making traditions. War-making against one's own people is a negation of all that principled policing stands for, whilst using police to make war at all is a negation of international standards exemplified in the Geneva Conventions where civil police are given the status of 'non-combatants' during war.

It follows therefore that although the police of the Weimar Republic might have developed an ethos of a democratic kind, they merely retained the traditional authoritarian ethos of military orthodoxy. If this is so, then it explains much concerning the apparent ease with which this orthodoxy served the excesses of Hitler's Reich. In Dieter Beese's words:

When the national socialism arose the traditional virtues were combined with the ideology of national socialism.[20]

The German military ethos was a most unsuitable one in the German context of the time since the leading Prussian military philosopher Carl von Clausewitz preached that '. . . to introduce into the philosophy of war a principle of moderation would be an absurdity. Two motives lead men to war: instinctive hostility and hostile intention'.[21] But these motives are not proper for police who should not think in terms of enemies.

The hostile intention of Hitler and his Nazi supporters towards the Jewish people was loudly proclaimed. Hitler '. . . spoke of the Jews in the most terrible manner cursing them with the most vile epithets. They were to be exterminated as a "pestilence"'.[22] The police therefore who swore to obey the Fuhrer in effect swore to exterminate the Jews and were thereby committed genocidists. 'Our constitution is the will of the Fuhrer',[23] said Hans Frank, Nazi lawyer, and it was this 'will' exemplified in the police command of SS Reichsfuhrer Heinrich Himmler which was to see the entire German police machine prepared for war and some notorious police formations prepared for the Holocaust. Oaths taken to obey the Fuhrer were to be fulfilled, catastrophically.

Police at war: 'Agents of genocide'[24]
On 1 September 1939, Hitler's military forces attacked Poland and the war had begun. The totalitarian police state had arrived.

The Order Police [ordnungspolizei], were as integral to the commission of the Holocaust as the Einsatzgruppen and the SS were. It was composed of the uniformed police [schutspolizei] under which police battalions operated, and the Gendarmerie [rural police]. Police battalions were the branch of the order police most intimately involved in the genocide. [25]

At the beginning of the war the order police of the German Reich under SS Reichsfuhrer Himmler numbered some 131,000 professional policemen, but their numbers reached around 310,000 by 1943 through 'raw draftees' who later formed the 'genocidal cohorts'. It was noted that whether the battalions were populated by professional policemen, reservists, or various combinations of these, they carried out their tasks of genocide 'in a manner which would have made Hitler proud'. [26]

Members of police battalions could have sought to be excused from genocidal operations, 'Jew killing of children, women, old people and defenceless civilians, but overwhelmingly decided to kill'. They had sworn to obey Hitler's every command, which of course included the plots and schemes of his rabid Nazi ministers. In any case, 'the Jew was not acknowledged by us to be a human being', the Order Police in Lublin implied. [27] In her report on Eichmann's trial in Jerusalem, Hannah Arendt observed that 'all officials of the police, not only of the Gestapo, but also of the Criminal Police and the Order Police, received SS titles corresponding to their previous ranks, regardless of whether or not they were party members. This meant that in the space of a day the most important part of the old civil services was incorporated into the most radical section of the Nazi heirarchy. No-one, so far as I know, protested, or resigned his job'. [29]

As mentioned in *Chapter 1* an account concerning one of the police battalions in Poland is graphically set out in Christopher Browning's book, *Ordinary Men* (see p.19), including the confession of a police officer who reasoned that it was in order for him to shoot a child once its mother had already been shot by his neighbour. [29]

Polizeistaat to totalitarian police state
The polizeistaat of Freidrich William (1621-88) and Fredrick II of Prussia (1712-86) is acknowledged to have been a utilitarian model of government set up to bring order and efficiency following a period of turbulence of the Thirty Years War and its aftermath.

The first Polizeistaat was therefore dedicated to three purposes: the protection of the population, the welfare of the state and its citizens, and the improvement of society. [30]

The state was all powerful and personified in the 'Prince'. In his lucid account, *Police State,* [31] Professor Chapman differentiates between the traditional, the modern, and the totalitarian models of the police state. The period of National Socialist Germany, from 1933 to 1939, during which German jurists and foreign observers recognised that Germany was a police state, he describes as a 'modern police state', to differentiate it from the 'traditional' poliziestaat of pre-Weimar Germany, and the ultimate, or 'totalitarian' police state which marked the German model between 1939 and 1945. The latter was a period of which Hans Frank, former minister of justice in Bavaria and Governor General of Poland under Hitler's Nazi regime, could say:

> as things are today when any citizen can be consigned to a concentration camp for any length of time without any possibility of redress, when there is no longer any security of life, freedom, honour, or honestly earned possessions, it is my firm conviction that any ethical relationship between the leadership of the state and its citizens is being totally destroyed. [32]

In 1946 Hans Frank was executed for war crimes following his trial at the Nuremburg Tribunal.

By now Hitler was able to defy the Army, the civil service was enmeshed by regulations, and both were bound by solemn oath to total obedience to Adolph Hitler. Now the police were omnipotent, for Himmler had brilliantly succeeded in achieving power beyond all others. But in Chapman's words,

> In attaining a position beyond their capacity to comprehend, the police became instruments of their own conceptions, the victims of their own apprehensions, and destroyers of all that the police stand for: law, morality, justice, and safety. [33]

INTERLUDE

It may be helpful, before proceeding further, to recap. At the beginning of the inquiry into principled policing contained in this chapter I recorded assertions that the professional police ethos was characteristically an amoral one, that the police ethic was indifferent to changing ideologies of governments, and that characteristics of unethical police stem from the very nature of police work itself.

The German experience appears to confirm—to a greater or lesser degree—that the foregoing assertions are proven. In case it may be thought that the German example is exceptional, I could also have chosen other examples including transference of the police of Czarist

Russia to the Communist Party of the Soviet Union, and now to democracy; or of the police of Imperial China to the rule of the Kuomintang, and now to the Chinese Communist Party. All these great and profound ideological changes would have required transference of professional police services from one to the other, the ideologies of which were diametrically opposed to those of their predecessors.

On a very much smaller and far less serious scale, we may observe incipient signs of the same adaptability of the police ethos in later chapters of this book.

I would suggest that it can be concluded from these inquiries so far that if society is to enjoy the services of the most ethical police, then there must be a cultural and political environment in which this state of affairs is rendered possible, and that is the issue which I would like to examine in *Part II* of this chapter.

PART II: WHAT ARE THE OPTIMUM CONDITIONS FOR HIGH ETHICAL POLICE?

The optimum conditions for the achievement of a high ethical standard of police would include the following:

1. A stable and sustainable liberal democracy.
2. A healthy vigorous civil-society, capable of providing a counter-balance to the power of government which, 'whilst not preventing the state from fulfilling its role as keeper of the peace, and arbitrator between major interests, can nevertheless prevent it from dominating and atomising the rest of society.' Bertrand Russell expressed the view that civil society was imperative 'to bring swift criticism to bear upon officials, police, magistrates, and judges, who exceed their powers', and that 'there is a danger to democracy in the fact that opinion in the police is far more reactionary than in the country at large'.[35]
3. A society in which there is a general sense of justice and fairness (as discussed earlier: see p. 30 *et al*)
4. A sense of tolerance for the 'Rule of Law,' (see p. 33) *only provided that the laws are the product of a free democracy and generally regarded as equitable and just by that society.* To seek to have unjust laws enforced by the police is to cause their ethical corruption.
5. A society in which there is an awareness of the propensity of police to lapse into unethical practices, which, as we have concluded, stem from the very nature of the policing function.

6. Acceptance of the principles of the Universal Declaration of Human Rights and Fundamental Freedoms.

In essence, a society cannot leave the question of ethical police to the police themselves—particularly where governments make use of the police for their own unethical gains, e.g. persecution of or discrimination against minorities.

The above characteristics of a society create conditions for ethical growth, but more has yet to be done to bring that growth about.

On securing an ethical police in optimum conditions
1. To secure an ethical police in optimum conditions it is necessary to provide a secure set of immutable principles upon which to base the policing function so that changing government policies may take place within a liberal democracy though the basic principles of policing remain entrenched, ideally in a constitution. But what are those so-called principles of police to be? An example can be found in the Constitution of the Federal Republic of Germany, viz:

Article 1 (Protection of Human Dignity)
(i) The dignity of man shall be inviolable. To respect and protect it shall be the duty of all state authority. [It is therefore a police duty]
(ii) The German people therefore acknowledge inviolable and inalienable Human Rights as the basis of every community, of peace and of justice in the world.

To express the police function as 'law enforcement' or 'keeping the peace', e.g. will not suffice, since both laws and the manner of their enforcement are neither immutable nor are they always just. 'Keeping the peace' can mean sustaining a tyrannical regime as has been noted in *Part I* of this chapter, and can mean the absence and diminution of freedom. The principles upon which to base ethical police should be those already described in *Chapter 1*, and which are driven by a notion of 'the common good'.

• • •

2. The laws are to be 'a covenant by which men assure one another of justice'. Thus the police are not a device to serve governments but to serve justice: the Kantian path to justice (see p. 33)

A police devoid of a sense and a spirit of justice is inimical to the healthy progress of democracy. In the words of John Rawls: 'Once the conception of justice is on hand, the ideas of respect, and of human

The police officers who made the system of Apartheid work were police officers under the previous regime.

The law of Apartheid enforced by the police diminished the freedom of trades unions, disenfranchised the minimum voting rights of Indian, black, and African people; and marriages between races, and sexual relations between black and white people were prohibited. Under the Group Areas Act 1950, racial groups were forbidden to live in the same urban areas. To give the police wider powers still, non-whites were required, under the infamous 'pass laws', to carry passes at all times, and failure to produce a pass when in a prohibited area—a i.e. white area— meant instant arrest. Black African lawyer Nelson Mandela, later activist for freedom and now the president of South Africa and a hero, describes his own life under Apartheid and his victimisation under the system in his personal account, *Long Walk to Freedom*.[38] Meanwhile the ethical corruption of the South African police was complete.

South Africa's long serving foreign minister Pik Botha, when giving evidence before the Truth and Reconciliation Commission, in October 1997, said that all South African cabinet ministers suspected the police were engaged in illegal activities including the killing and torturing of the government's opponents. He regretted that they had not done more to stop this;[39] a question of a failure of moral leadership, a subject to which I will now turn.

Ethics and police leaders
In societies where the ethics of government and of public life are high it would be expected that the ethics of police leadership would also be high, but, as will be noted in subsequent chapters, where policies of government fall short of high ethical standards, police leaders can find themselves facing a dilemma. At times, the failure of politics to provide justice can lead to public disorder and even to terrorism.

One of the main aims of terrorism is to discredit a system of government which it opposes by inducing over-reaction on the part of the police and the criminal justice system, and thereby gaining moral support, and condemnation of the police and government. Terrorism might be called 'the great corrupter of police and justice', since it occupies a space between peace and war, and there are no specific rules to deal with it. Police know their lawful operational boundaries in peace, and soldiers know their rules and conventions in war, but terrorism and counter-terrorism is neither of these.

One writer on terrorism argues that '. . . an operative liberal democratic society must learn to afford and tolerate high levels of protest, turbulence and extra Parliamentary agitation'. Sounding a note of caution, the same commentator says, 'If liberal governments and societies try to suppress or ignore deeply felt needs and grievances then peaceful protests and agitation and passive civil disobedience are likely to give way rapidly to political violence'.[40]

It is important for police to maintain their high ethical standards when facing terrorism, and for their leaders to inspire resistance to any degeneration into counter-terrorism, terror.

Article 3 of the European Convention of Human Rights provides that 'No-one shall be subjected to torture or to inhuman or degrading treatment or punishment'. Delivering its verdict on the use of illegal methods of interrogation in contravention of article 3 by security services seeking to combat terrorism, the European Court of Human Rights said '. . . even in the longest and most violent campaign witnessed' (Northern Ireland), in a 'tragic and lasting crisis' there can be no diminution of this fundamental and immutable provision.[41] The interrogation techniques involved in this case—which included the hooding of prisoners, deprivation of sleep, food, drink, and subjection to noise, and 'wall standing' in stress positions—were approved, it was conceded, 'at a high level'. Once again, this raises the question of the ethics of police leadership.

Consideration of police ethics seems almost invariably to be expressed in terms of the behaviour of police officers in the lower ranks, and seldom, if ever, those of the high police and others in leadership positions. Police officers may, and *should*, refuse to obey orders which are unlawful, as provided for in the UN Code of Conduct for Law Enforcement Officials, and in the European Declaration on the Police, and sometimes in domestic laws and regulations. But their leaders should never have given these orders in the first place. I would suggest that this problem may be approached by the provision of a code of ethics for police leaders. If so, what might such a code say? The following can be suggested as a starting point:

Police leadership: A declaration
I will seek to inculcate high ethical humanitarian standards into carrying out of duties by officers under my command, whilst at the same time accepting their need to use force, sometimes deadly force, in the lawful performance of duty, and the need to use powers granted to us by governments so that we may protect the people, their freedoms, and their property, in accordance with the spirit of the implied social contract.

I will not ask, demand of, or cause any officer under my command to carry out duties and actions which are contrary to the laws of my country, or to those laws of international covenants and treaties such as the Universal Declaration of Human Rights and its protocols, and the European

71

Principled Policing
Convention on Human Rights and Fundamental Freedoms which have been
adopted by my government.

All this I promise in the cause of justice, freedom and the common good.

All police officers: A declaration
I acknowledge my moral and legal obligations under the implied social
contract between myself, the government and the people. In accordance
with my social contractual obligations I will strive to protect and safeguard
the lives, safety, freedoms and property of all people with equal regard, and
all this in the cause of justice and the spirit of the common good.

I know that I am not obliged to carry out any order which is contrary to the
laws of my country, and contrary to any international treaty and protocol
adopted by the government of my country.

At all times when discharging my lawful duties I will seek to do so in an
ethical manner upholding both the letter and spirit of those laws which
protect the human rights of all the people without exception.

Human Rights and the police
In the 1940s when I became a police officer the vocabulary of police did
not contain or acknowledge 'Human Rights', though gradually the
theory of basic rights emerged to touch the policing function following
the establishment of the United Nations Organization and the
publication and impact of the Universal Declaration of Human Rights in
1948.

The Universal Declaration was the first great human enterprise to
claim for all people in the world their birthrights (the League of Nations
had not succeeded in this regard). In providing for Human Rights in this
way a duty lay at the door of all governments and their police
institutions to secure and protect them.

Although that great eighteenth century English expositor of the
political philosophy of utilitarianism, Jeremy Bentham, described the
idea of rights as 'nonsense' and natural rights as 'nonsense on stilts'
there is now little doubt that the philosophy of governments of recent
times has witnessed a shift from utility to rights (*Chapter 1*). In the words
of a leading philosopher of our time, H L A Hart, 'We are currently
witnessing, I think, the progress of a transition from a once widely
accepted old faith that some form of utlitarianism . . . must capture the
essence of political morality. The new faith is that the truth must lie not
with a doctrine that takes maximisation of aggregate or average general
welfare for its good, but with a doctrine of basic Human Rights
protecting the specific basic liberties of individuals . . . '[42]

72

For the police, this shift from utility to rights has very important ethical implications.

Police: The Human Rights mission

Declarations, covenants, conventions, codes, resolutions and protocols mark the steady march across the international landscape of concern for human rights.[43]

The Universal Declaration of Human Rights was adopted and proclaimed by the General Assembly of the United Nations in resolution 217 A (111) on 10 December 1948.

The European Convention on Human Rights and Fundamental Freedoms was signed by member states on 4 November 1950. The Convention was drawn up with the aim of taking 'the first steps for the collective enforcement of certain of the rights stated in the Universal Declaration'. The police are at the centre of the struggle and desire of peoples to acquire and retain their human birthrights.

Free people and their less fortunate counterparts expect much of their police, but in free societies the police stand at the point of balance, on the one hand securing Human Rights whilst, on the other, exercising their lawful powers given to them by governments in the name of the people—to protect the people and their institutions.

Societies which are not free, or which are despotic, acquire omnipotent police who serve only those in power. Laws are sometimes promulgated which give the police the widest of powers to deny Human Rights, in some cases even basic civil liberties. Police in corrupt systems are themselves corrupted. But the police in the world are not neatly or distinctly divided into two forms, for there are degrees of both.

Police authority can be abused even in democracies. It can become more the master and less the servant, snuffing out more freedom than is protected. The main problem lies in the powers and controls of unsympathetic regimes, and this is particularly the case in the growth and the practice of secret police. It is important to remember that abuses flourish not only through official negligence or indifference but because rightly or wrongly, and often wrongly, broad sections of the people identify with such practices. People consider that in spite of their excesses the police are carrying out a necessary and unpleasant task if both state and society are to be preserved and protected. Such a situation, great or small, places considerable moral burdens on decent police officials who seek to check drifts of this kind which are so important in the preservation of Human Rights.

From rebellion to simple theft there are requirements for laws and for their enforcement, for human experience tells us that noble sentiments alone are too weak to control those whose ambitions, greed, aggression and anger lead on to threatening and damaging activity on both small and grand scales.

In creating police instruments, free societies have to take great care on two counts; firstly, they have to ensure that the system created for their protection does not become the instrument of their bondage; secondly it is in the protection of basic freedoms—enshrined in domestic laws and internal declarations and conventions—that the primary object of advanced policing is to be found, and this in accord with the 'theory of protectionism' discussed in *Chapter 1*.

Endnotes

1. United Nations, 'Universal Declaration of Human Rights'
2. Champion, B, *Police State*, Macmillan: London, p. 93
3. Ibid, p. 96
4. Lipset, M L, *New Society*, 6 March 1969
5. Alderson, J C, and Stead, P J, (Eds), *The Police We Deserve*, Wolfe: London, 1973
6. Browder, G C, *Hitler's Enforcers*, Oxford University Press: New York, 1990
7. Bullock, A, *Hitler: A Study in Tyranny*, Penguin: London, 1962, p. 57
8. Dokumentation: 2, Europaisches, Polizei und Kirche, Frankfurt am Main, 8 to 12 May 1995
9. Hohne, H, *The Order of the Death's Head*, Pan: London, 1972, p. 81
10. Ibid, p. 164
11. Ibid, p. 496
12. Ibid, p. 163
13. Padfield, P, *Himmler*, Papermac: London, 1991, p. 144
14. Bullock, op. cit. p. 385
15. Padfield, op. cit. p. 127
16. Ibid, p. 185
17. Ibid, p. 197
18. Fosdick, R, *European Police Systems*, The Century Company: New York, 1915, p. 205
19. Pulzer, P, *Germany 1870-1945*, Oxford University Press, 1997, p. 79
20. 'Codes of Ethics for the Police in Germany', Paper delivered at Council of Europe Seminar, Strasbourg, June 1996
21. Clausewitz, C von, *On War*, Penguin: London, 1968, p. 102
22. Bullock, op. cit., p. 407
23. Ibid, p. 403
24. Goldhagen, D J, *Hitler's Willing Executioners*, Little, Brown and Co: London, 1996
25. Ibid, p. 181
26. Ibid, p. 274
27. Ibid, p. 280
28. Arendt, H, *Eichman in Jerusalem*, Penguin: London, 1994, p. 68
29. Browning, C R, *Ordinary Men*, Harper Collins: New York, 1992, p. 72/73
30. Chapman op. cit., p. 16
31. Op. cit.
32. Op. cit., p. 110
33. Op. cit., p. 115
34. Gellner, E, *Conditions of Liberty*, Hamish Hamilton: London, 1994
35. Russell, B, *Power*, Unwin Books: London, 1975, p. 192
36. Rawls, op. cit. p. 586
37. UNESCO, *Apartheid*, Paris, 1972, p. 24
38. Mandela, N, *Long Walk to Freedom*, Little, Brown and Co: London, 1994

39. *The Guardian,* 15 October 1997
40. European Court of Human Rights, 18 January 1978, Series A, No. 25
41. Critchley, T A, *The History of Police in England and Wales,* Constable: London, 1968
42. Ryan, A (Ed), *The Idea of Freedom*, Oxford University Press, 1979, p. 79
43. Alderson, J, *Human Rights and the Police*, Council of Europe, Strasbourg, 1984.

Part II

Theory Into Practice

CHAPTER 4

Moral Failure, Disorder and Police

I suggested at the beginning of *Chapter 2* that public disorder on a significant scale was an indicator of moral failure, but that this may sometimes be inevitable. Large scale disorder may even take place in a society which is based on the theory of justice as fairness, since people and their institutions lack perfection.

Minimising damage
Even when disorder becomes inevitable it should be the aim of high police to ensure the minimum amount of damage to the social fabric, since to do this accrues to the common good. The excessive use of force will not easily be reconcilable with the people's peace in the aftermath of disorder. It is both wrong, and imprudent, to sow the 'dragon's teeth' of future violence, as well as being contrary to the spirit of the social contract and its laws. The doctrine of the use of minimum force is of great importance to the morality of principled policing, a subject which I turn to in later chapters. It is against the background of all that may be said of theory that I now turn to some practical instances.

DOMESTIC POLICING AND THE VIETNAM WAR

The Vietnam War was a defining cause of public agitation particularly in US society, but also throughout societies in the free world. It should be stressed that we are not here concerned with US involvement in the war in Vietnam as such, but we are concerned with the war as the cause of civil disobedience and public disorder. I will mention confrontations between people, mainly students, and police, and the degree and causes of violence, in order to test theories which we have, or will have, expressed.

In 1995, Robert McNamara, US secretary of defense from 1961 to 1967, expressed his deep regret at the failure of US Presidents to disengage from deeper and deeper involvement in this Asian quagmire, and its terrible cost in human lives and resources. By 1967 he regarded the war as a lost cause: 'We were wrong, terribly wrong',[1] he said. Others expressed misgivings, doubts, and regrets as one might expect in a liberal democracy.

'Vietnam syndrome'
Henry Kissinger said: 'It has poisoned our domestic debate'.[2] '[President] Johnson sensed that the war was poisoning his administration'.[3] 'The war polarised the American people and poisoned the political debate as had no issue since slavery'.[4] '. . . the most unpopular in its [the USA's] history'.[5] '. . . millions of Americans had been searching for a real meaningful way to put an end to the war they thought was immoral and illegal'.[6] 'But whether a valid venture or a misguided endeavour it was a tragedy of epic dimensions'.[7] 'The basic issue remains the morality and wisdom of intervention in Vietnam'.[8]

The foregoing selection of comments could be multiplied many times to portray the anguish of a nation caught up in a cause regarded by millions of people as wrong, and by many as a poisonous and immoral disaster. Many others argued in favour of the war in defence of freedom and democracy over the encroachment of communism. In a critical memorandum to President Johnson in May 1967, Robert McNamara wrote,

> The Vietnam War is unpopular in this country. The picture of the world's greatest superpower killing or injuring 1,000 non-combatants a week, while trying to pound a tiny backward nation into submission on an issue whose merits are hotly disputed, is not a pretty one.[9]

Those of us who were senior police officers in many western nations at the time were very aware of the threat to the people's peace which anti-Vietnam War protesters, along with the general turbulence on university campuses, posed. From the foregoing comments it is clear that we were witnessing moral failure alongside youthful idealism. This, I believe, gives further support to the theory that public protest and disorder on a significant scale is always an indication of moral failure.

Dissent
Dissenters to the laws compelling young men into service in the US Armed Forces for the Vietnam War based their objections on the following moral and legal grounds:[10]

a) The United States is using immoral weapons and tactics in Vietnam.
b) The war has never been endorsed by deliberate, considered, and open vote of the people's representatives.

c) The United States has no interest at stake in Vietnam remotely strong enough to justify forcing a segment of its citizens to risk death there.

d) If an army is to be raised to fight that war it is immoral to raise it by a draft which defers college students, and thus discriminates against the economically under-privileged.

e) The draft exempts those who object to all wars on religious grounds, but not those who object to particular wars on moral grounds; there is no relevant difference between these positions, and so the draft by making the distinction implies that the second group is less worthy of the nation's respect than the first.

f) The law that makes it a crime to counsel draft resistance stifles those who oppose war, because it is morally impossible to argue that the war is profoundly immoral, without encouraging those who refuse to fight it.

Protest in action

We now seem to have a war which is widely regarded as immoral, and a system of conscription which is also described as immoral. As we approach the prospect of protest, civil disobedience and disorder, we must examine the next stage—being the manner in which protest on moral grounds will be dealt with by the authorities.

As any police officer will know, there is a degree of apprehension, uncertainty, and tension within the ranks as preparations are made for the policing of protest. The maintenance of high morale will depend very much on cohesion and mutual support. It is a time for cool and informed leadership, and meticulous briefing. Unless they are well trained, and in particular have absorbed the virtue of self-restraint and control under provocation, police officers will find it difficult to maintain the principled policing which is especially important on these occasions. The testing time will come.

Conflict in Chicago: August 1968

The issue most immediately relevant to Convention Week in Chicago was the war in Vietnam. [11]

The Democratic National Convention of 1968 took place in Chicago from August 25 to 29. It was an occasion which became notorious for the nature of its police violence, not in an organized, disciplined fashion but on the contrary: 'To a shocking extent they consisted of crowd-police battles in the parks as well as in the streets. And the shock was

81

intensified by the presence in the crowds by large numbers of dissenting citizens'.[12]

It was these dissenting citizens who, in the main, were there to protest about the war in Vietnam. An official observer from the Los Angeles Police Department, whilst praising the police restraint on the early days of the week, said of the police action on the Wednesday:

> There is no question but that many officers acted without restraint, and exerted force beyond that necessary under the circumstances. *The leadership at the point of conflict did little to prevent such conduct, and the direct control of officers by first-line supervision was virtually non-existent.*[13] (Emphasis supplied).

There is evidence of official apprehension caused by threats of disorder, violence, and even the bizarre threat of the contamination of the city's water supply with the drug LSD.

The Walker Report considered that the portents of violence were foreshadowed long before Convention Week arrived, and described them in the following terms:

> These were: threats to the city; the city's response; and the conditioning of Chicago Police that violence against demonstrators as against rioters would be condoned by city officials.[14]

To treat peaceful demonstrators, even when provocative, as one would treat rioters, is not only morally wrong, but it is unconstitutional—since the right to peaceful protest is guaranteed under the US Constitution. The climate for violence was given much impetus by reckless comments from the mayor after the riots in Chicago following the murder of Martin Luther King earlier in 1968. The police had generally been praised for the restraint which they had exhibited on this occasion, but the mayor, Richard J Daley, publicly rebuked the city's police chief and issued a widely disseminated and illegal order that the city police should 'shoot to kill arsonists, and shoot to maim looters'. This order, it was said, was later modified, though it must have had a damaging effect amongst the ranks of the police on duty, for whom the message was clearly intended to go over the head of their publicly rebuked chief. Political direction in police operations is much more common in the US than in Britain, where the professional high police have a considerable measure of independence in these matters.

The effect of the mayor's order was to be manifest some weeks later when the police 'attacked demonstrators, bystanders, and media representatives' at the Civic Centre peace march. There was published criticism, but the city's response was to ignore the police violence.[15] In the words of the Walker Report, 'Government—federal, state and local—moved to defend itself from the threats, both imaginary and real'. The preparations included: US Army personnel carriers under secret service control; 6,000 Regular Army troops in full gear, equipped with rifles, flame throwers and bazookas; and 6,000 National Guard with rifles, bayonets, and gas being mobilised to assist the 12,000 police officers of the Chicago Police Department.

Although prudent high police would always make sure that likely eventualities were covered, there seems to have been a heady cocktail brewing up before the Convention Week arrived. In what was a mistaken strategy, the city officials '. . . attempted to discourage an inundation of demonstrators by not granting permits for marches and rallies', whilst threatening that the law against non-approved marches and rallies would be strictly enforced. If this was meant to deter people from attending the protests and rallies it certainly failed. The estimated 10,000 visiting protesters who stayed in the parks during the day holding meetings and rallies were each evening cleared out on to the streets where further disorder took place, generated by the ensuing chaos which in turn provoked police anger and seriously inconvenienced both pedestrians and motorists. It would have been far better for all concerned, and for control of the situation, had permits been granted to all the leaders of the varying factions, for in this way crowd movement would have been predictable and leaders more accountable.

The compendious crowd—as on all these occasions included some offensive, disorderly and violent rabble, which further generated police reaction. As so often happens, a minority of offensive people provides the opportunity for stereotyping all the protesters as being of this kind. This was a grave mistake, since the overwhelming majority were there peacefully to protest about the Vietnam War, and the current state of society generally. Stereotyping gives the police *carte blanch* to treat everyone as if they are extremists and anti-social.

After the first three days of the conference the street violence and disorder of the people met the counter violence of the police. Angry young people and tired frustrated police officers were in regular confrontation and in skirmishes, but the culmination of violence was recorded on Wednesday August 28, the penultimate day of the Democratic National Convention. In the early morning, protesters were cleared from the park by police to facilitate the clearing of rubbish. Some of the protesters joined the cleaners to help, and were given sticks with nails in the end with which to do this (ideal weapons) which were seen in action later that day.

A crowd began to build up across the road from the Hilton Hotel to an estimated 8,000 to 10,000, large enough to need policing with adequate caution to avoid stampede and riot. As on all occasions of this kind, it only needs a spark to detonate the latent smouldering desire for violence; violence by both demonstrators and police. On this occasion the spark came in the form of a young man who climbed a flag pole to lower the stars and stripes. This so angered the police that a small group were sent in amongst the restive crowd of, by now, some 15,000 people. 'If the crowd had meant business it would have killed these men', said a *New York Times* reporter in his statement to the Walker inquiry.

The police were pelted with stones, bricks, planks, chunks of concrete, cans, bottles, and perhaps some smoking rags. They regrouped on the fringe of the crowd whilst a leader of the protest sought to calm them through the use of megaphone messages, and marshalls strove to push the crowd back from the police. The crowd moved back as a line of police approached and began 'indiscriminate beating of a large number of people' (a matron); '. . . the police hit and shoved whoever was in their path, men, women, clergymen, newsmen; some were beaten and clubbed while on the ground' (an attorney). 'As the police broke rank and carried out individual actions, one began hitting an older lady'. Both police and demonstrators suffered injuries. This kind of violence continued throughout the afternoon. Marshalls sought to negotiate a peaceful march to the conference centre known as the Amphitheatre. The march, 5,000 to 6,000 strong was stopped by police, and the marchers began to sit down on the sidewalk. No arrests were made. After about an hour of negotiation the protesters were refused permission to march and told to go back to the parks. The dangers of an aimless, leaderless, wandering and frustrated crowd of this size constituted an unpredictable threat to public order.

The National Guard (now called in) came under pressure and began to spray gas on the crowd: '. . . hundreds of people running, crying, coughing, vomitting, screaming'. Huge traffic jams built up, and from this point onwards free floating violence from some less peaceful protesters, and savage beatings of people by police were reported incessantly from many areas of the district. At around 8.00 p.m., groups of club-wielding police converged and 'battle was joined'. The deputy superintendent of police has been described by observers as being very upset with individual policemen who beat demonstrators. This whole episode has been described as 'a police riot'.

And so the peaceful protest desired by the National Mobilisation Committee to end the War in Vietnam failed as the whole sorry affair drew to a close. A high price has been paid for strategic and tactical errors on the part of the authorities, and by the wild behaviour of some of the protesters. Official statistics (see the Walker Report) recorded 192 police officers injured, forty-nine hospitalised. Known injuries to demonstrators were 1,025, plus 102 hospitalised.

Killings at Kent State[16]

The events which took place at Kent State University, Ohio, USA, in early May 1970 provide us with another example of disorder generated by the Vietnam War protest. The University was not immune from the turbulence which characterised western universities in the 1960s and 1970s. In 1968 there had been a protest on the campus against police recruiting teams, and, in 1969, 58 students had been arrested for 'disrupting campus activities'. Campuses at the time were politicised particularly concerning racial injustice, individual freedom, including recreational use of drugs, but it was the hyper-sensitivity over the US involvement in the Vietnam War which made them a political threat to the established order.

At this time I was chief constable of Devon and Cornwall, England, and I received a visit from the vice-chancellor of the local university who expressed the wish that I would consider sending police officers on to the campus to control the behaviour of some undergraduates which was causing concern. The students were breaking into offices, examining their files and reports, staging sit-ins, and generally disrupting university life and its routines.

I was sympathetic, but counselled the vice-chancellor against my sending police officers on to a university campus, on the grounds that it would make matters worse rather than better, unless serious criminal behaviour was taking place. I was anxious that there would be no legacy of bitterness and regret. After all, I pointed out, the undergraduates were not trespassers, but were members of the university, with more right to be on the campus than I had. I suggested that their non-criminal behaviour was a matter for the university.

As it turned out over time, the campus gradually returned to normal, and happily there were no hostages to fortune. If that was the position in England, it was much more acute in the US. It seems that at Kent State University the students and some faculty members were heavily politicised. The pattern of events which took place falls into seven phases:

85

1. On Thursday 30 April 1970, President Nixon broadcast to the nation announcing that US troops were to invade Cambodia for strategic purposes.
2. On the following day a group of undergraduates arranged a rally of protest which was attended by some 500 students and members of the faculty, and they made speeches condemning the president's action. Another non-violent rally was arranged for Monday May 4.
3. Public disorder broke out in downtown Kent that evening which caused damage to shop windows, some looting and general crowd violence. Police reinforcements were called in and 15 people arrested. The mayor of Kent proclaimed a state of civil emergency. It was not established that this disorder was led by university students nor were any of those arrested from Kent.
4. Events on Saturday, May 2 indicated official apprehension. The state governor arbitrarily ordered an 8.00 p.m. curfew for students, and without any warning called out the National Guard. The guards occupied the university campus without any consultation with the President, who did not want them on the premises. Groups of students were assaulted with tear gas by the guards and treated by them with contempt. That night, the university's Reserve Officers' Training Corps building on the campus was burned.
5. On Monday May 4, National Guardsmen on the campus threw tear gas bombs towards groups of students, who were moving around the grounds as classes were in session. The students taunted the guards and some threw back the bombs. Shortly afterwards, some members of the National Guard fired their rifles indiscriminately amongst students around the grounds, killing four, and wounding seven.
6. None of the students who were killed or wounded was in any way connected with disorderly behaviour.
7. Political deception followed with the alleged rigging of a grand jury. No-one was ever indicted for killing or wounding these innocent people.

In reaching an understanding of this regrettable affair, we are fortunate in having access to the full text of the US Justice Department's confidential summary of the FBI findings of what happened on the campus on the days in question.[17] It was reported:

We have some reason to believe that the claim by the National Guard that their lives were endangered by the students was fabricated subsequent to the event.

The politics of the aftermath of the killings are of importance since we are concerned with the morality of the entire sequence of events. Senator Stephen Young of Ohio, writing the foreword to Stone's book, points out that in a television interview with David Frost, Vice-President Agnew, who would have had access to the FBI Reports, voiced the opinion that the National Guard had committed murder at Kent State. On the other hand, Senator Young bluntly criticises the Portage County Special Grand Jury Investigation as a 'fraud from the start'.[18] He also alleges that the jury was summoned by the state attorney-general, who was a political friend of the governor, he who had sent in the National Guard to a boisterous, but non-violent campus.

The grand jury proceedings were also directed by the governor's political chums, one of whom was the chairman of the County Republican party who said '. . . the National Guard should have shot all the trouble makers'. To define a 'trouble maker' as deserving of being killed is an outrageous idea and totally void of morality.

The grand jury did not indict one guardsman out of those responsible for the killings, but they did indict 25 students and one professor!

The final damning of this political chicanery was revealed after a lengthy investigation by the President's Commission on Campus Unrest which concluded:

Even if guardsmen faced danger it was not a danger which called for lethal force. The 61 shots by 28 guardsmen certainly cannot be justified . . .

In the matter of principled policing, the whole sorry sequence of events which took place at Kent State University on those fateful days in May 1970 provides many lessons. The doctrine of minimum force was certainly breached, as was the United Nations Code of Conduct for Law Enforcement Officials, article 3, which states and requires:

. . . the use of firearms is considered an extreme measure. Every effort should be made to exclude the use of firearms . . . in general firearms should not be used except when a suspected offender offers armed resistance, or otherwise jeopardises the lives of others and less extreme measures are not sufficient to restrain or apprehend the suspected offender.

The FBI investigation concluded that most of the National Guardsmen who did fire their weapons did not claim that it was because their lives were in danger. Meanwhile the Vietnam War protest movement was spreading, and those of us concerned with the policing of London at the time were beginning to anticipate its impact on the people's peace there.

London 1968[19]

The first manifestation of anti-Vietnam War protest in London took place on Sunday, 17 March 1968. The Vietnam Solidarity Campaign, though mainly a British affair, also included international elements. This was a time when the rising generation of students and young people generally—in the USA, Europe, Japan, and elsewhere—was very restive and prone to protest and demonstrate over a whole range of dissatisfaction with the post-war society of which they were the progeny.

On March 17, some 7,000 protesters gathered in London's Trafalgar Square where they were addressed by their leaders before marching to the US Embassy in Grosvenor Square. About 2,000 people were already in Grosvenor Square when the main procession arrived. Groups of protesters sought to gain entry to the US Embassy and this resulted in serious disorder. Mounted police detachments, which had been assembled out of sight behind the embassy, were summoned to push back protesters to relieve foot police cordons which were in danger of being overwhelmed. As the mounted police detachments moved into position, some panic amongst demonstrators took place.

This manoeuvre of the mounted police was later accepted to have been a mistake, and that in future such detachments were to remain in view of protesters to deter them, rather than reacting to events. Another lesson which was learned here was that it is tactically unwise to allow large numbers of people who are demonstrating to march into an area which does not have adequate outlets and means of escaping the pressure building up behind. On this day, 155 police officers were injured and 42 demonstrators received minor injuries; some damage was done to property.

The anti-Vietnam War protest was not the only one in London in 1968. Large scale public demonstrations, usually of a reasonably non-violent kind, concerned such matters as the anti-Apartheid movement vis-à-vis South Africa, the Campaign for Nuclear Disarmament, the Rhodesian civil war, and others. Though the great majority of the people demonstrating were sincere and pacific there were, as happens in most large scale and otherwise peaceful demonstrations, opportunist forces seeking to use violence for its own sake, or for narrow anti-democratic motives.

It takes a good deal of disciplined restraint, and good judgment on the part of principled police to avoid using the violent behaviour of a few as an excuse for characterising the peaceful majority in the same mould, and as a justification for the use of police violence generally, as was witnessed in Chicago (see p. 81).

In the London scenario at the time, there were small and rebellious groups describing themselves as Maoists (following the Chinese communist pattern), Trotskyists (revolutionary communists), and anarchists. These movements were subject to surveillance in view of their propensity for creating disorder out of all proportion to their numbers. The Commissioner of Police for the Metropolis at the time, Sir John Waldron, considered that 'in spite of this threatened violence and the inconvenience these marches create, I would always support the right of peaceful demonstration', and prudently, '. . . if this were limited or curtailed the ban would unite many of those who at the moment have opposing policies'.

The anticipated scale of the anti-Vietnam War demonstrations, and the evidence of violence from the USA, and the European continent, were to test these liberal sentiments of London's commissioner of police to the full. Those of us who were amongst his senior officers supported his sentiments, which were admirable in the context of London at the time, when he declared:

> I take the view that we should deal with violent demonstrations by traditional methods, that the man in the front row of a police cordon may be working a foot patrol on the day before and the day after he is called up for this special duty; that we do not wear protective clothing, and do not make use of tear gas, water cannon, barbed wire barriers, or any equipment that could be said to give rise to provocation to the demonstrators.

This is a policy which was the outcome of a cultural tradition and custom of the police and of the people in these matters, and which manifested an understanding of mutual obligation of the right to demonstrate on the one hand and the duty to keep the peace on the other. Some voices were raised in Parliament against this traditional tolerance being of the view that disruptive street demonstrations were no longer a necessary political outlet since there were ample opportunities through which to register protest such as the media and meeting places. I have never supported this view, but there is a price to pay for tolerance of active street protest, including the risk of the failure of policing strategy. The commissioner explained:

> In order to keep the temperature cool and prevent the battle [sic] from escalating, the men have to show a tremendous restraint, for they are pushed, kicked, abused and insulted, and once again I would pay tribute to the loyalty, forbearance, patience and good humour that officers of all ranks have displayed in the face of considerable provocation . . . Success has been achieved by the fine example of steadiness and good sense that the Metropolitan Police have shown and one can be very proud of them.

This all seems to be a far cry from the bellicose language of the political authorities in Chicago and Kent State, USA, during public protests around the same time—but of course as has been emphasised the context of time and place in which events happen has to be allowed for.

The occurrence of large events and of angry protest with minimum violence only serves to emphasise an underlying semblance of an instinctive social contractual spirit. The people have an obligation to eschew violence, which is a crime, and without doubt the police have similar obligations. Should the police initiate violence they not only commit crime, but they forfeit the moral right not to have violence turned upon themselves. Unnecessary police violence is in breach of the theory of the social contract.

Advance publicity concerning the London Vietnam Solidarity Campaign predicted a protest by crowds of up to 100,000 people on the 26 and 27 October 1968. In the event, crowds were assessed to be upwards of 30,000. Though smaller than predicted, it was still a considerable number should the crowd become violent, and it was greater than the Chicago crowds around the same time. In the previous year a crowd in New York estimated at 100,000 protesting the war in Vietnam passed off without undue violence, but in this case, unlike that of Chicago, the authorities had issued permits to the various organizations involved; which is a point worth noting.

In his report to the secretary of state on the outcome of the London anti-Vietnam War demonstration of 27 October 1968, the commissioner reported that some 25,000 to 30,000 demonstrators assembled and marched through London. The main procession continued into Whitehall where a petition was handed in to the prime minister's office at 10 Downing Street. One or two minor disorders took place before the main body continued to Hyde Park for speeches and a rally. Some 1,000 protesters marched on the United States Embassy in Grosvenor Square; this had been anticipated by the police planners and the embassy was protected by a cordon of foot and mounted police. Some violence took place when demonstrators and police clashed. Seventy-four police officers and 47 members of the public were injured, and 42 people arrested. The operation was policed by 9,000 police officers, approximately one police officer to every three demonstrators, a very high proportion of police, but of course they had no anti-riot equipment or personal body protection.

On 19 November 1968, the House of Commons unanimously carried a resolution congratulating the police for their '. . . efficiency, good discipline, and tolerance under great provocation'. On November 6, the Greater London Council presented a roll of 300,000 signatures from the public congratulating the police on their 'tact, restraint, and good humour during the demonstration'.

Writing in *The Sunday Times* the following week,[20] Mary McCarthy stated 'This was a unique improbable event, something to cherish in our memory book, for, short of Utopia, we shall not see it again'. Foreign observers were equally impressed, their views being typically represented by the London correspondent of the *Washington Post* who described the outcome as 'a moral example', and one 'of potent appeal to the world. British experience in building a non-violent relatively gentle society seems of paramount importance to a world beset by police brutality and student nihilism'.[21]

We should take the London event of 27 October 1968 as a very good example of the importance of traditional expectations built up over a period of time during which the people do not expect to be violently attacked by police when exercising their right of dissent—and the police in turn do not anticipate being attacked by the people. No riot squads or any equipment was on display or available. It was a triumph of civic morality.

It should be noted that one feature which differed between the Chicago disorders and the London demonstrations, was that in Chicago the political officials could be said to have declared a campaign of deterrence on the demonstrators, in the hope that they would be discouraged from attending and taking part. The officials were proved to have been unwise and mistaken.

When the Chicago demonstrators arrived, the police authorities had no way of effectively accommodating their presence and were left with no alternative but to seek their control by force, rather than by consent. In London, on the other hand, the demonstrators wishes were accommodated; routes were marked out to facilitate the procession, and a final meeting place where the demonstration could terminate in an orderly manner was provided. This lesson had been learned in London out of experience and the Hyde Park riots of 1867, where a demonstration became violent for the same reasons as it did in Chicago in 1968. By Act of Parliament, Hyde Park was designated as a legitimate meeting place for public protest.

91

At the end of this brief comment on what I will call 'Vietnam War Syndrome'—its impact on the people's peace in the USA and elsewhere—it might reasonably be concluded that public disorder on a large scale results from moral failure.

Endnotes

1. McNamara, R and Van Der Mark, B, *In Retrospect: The Tragedy and Lessons of Vietnam*, Times Books: New York, 1995
2. Karnow, S, *Vietnam: A History*, Penguin: London, 1984, p. 9
3. Ibid. p. 479
4. Herring, G C, *America's Longest War*, Second Edition, McGraw Hill: New York, 1986, p. 256
5. Wells, J M (Ed.), *The People v. Providential War*, Dunellen: New York, 1970, p. 2
6. Ibid, p. 41
7. Karnow, op. cit. p. 11
8. Herring, op. cit. p. 276
9. McNamara, op. cit. p. 269
10. Dworkin, R, *Taking Rights Seriously*, Duckworth: London, 1977, p. 208
11. Walker, *Rights in Conflict*, Bantam Books: New York, 1968, p. 14 This is an excellent source of 356 pages including a summary of the plans concerning the protest and a comprehensive account of the disorders.
12. Ibid, p. 4 *et. seq*
13. Ibid, p. 2
14. Ibid, pp. 2-3
15. Ibid, p. 3
16. Stone, I F, 'The Killings at Kent State', *New York Review*, 1970. This is a most helpful source, and I have relied on it. It includes the full text of the Justice Department's secret summary of FBI findings, and there is an interesting introduction by Senator Young of Ohio.
17. Ibid, p. 84
18. Ibid, Introduction by Senator Young of Ohio
19. Report of the Commissioner of Police of the Metropolis 1968, Cmnd. 4060, HMSO: London
20. *Sunday Times*, 4 November 1968
21. *The Times*, 30 October 1968.

CHAPTER 5

Disorder and Police in a Not Well-Ordered Society

In this and the next chapter, I propose to consider some of the fundamental characteristics of the nature of social order, and their implications for the policing function.

NORTHERN IRELAND 1968 - 1972

There are many traps for the unwary when considering the condition of the social order in Northern Ireland; I believe, however, that examination of it can be very instructive when considering principled policing. I have therefore chosen the social order in Northern Ireland in the period 1968 to 1972 against which to consider the Rawlsian concept of the 'well-ordered' society, and its policing.

A well-ordered society
John Rawls considers a well-ordered society to be one

> . . . designed to advance the good of its members [all of its members] and effectively regulated by a public conception of justice

It is one in which 'everyone accepts and know that others accept the same principles of justice'. We might take note here of the contractual character of this principle, and of its reflection of an earlier consideration of one of the characteristics of principled policing, that is the 'theory of protectionism' wherein the law is considered to be a 'covenant by which men assure one another of justice' and the state 'a co-operative association for the prevention of crime' (see page 25).

The second element of Rawl's concept of 'the well-ordered society' is one in which 'basic social institutions satisfy and are know to satisfy these principles', i.e. the good of all its members and a conception of justice. The laws, the police, and the courts are 'the basic social institutions' of the greatest importance. Should these institutions fail to satisfy the aforementioned principles of justice, their effectiveness in helping to maintain adequate institutional 'stability' in a democratic society would be vitiated. A well-ordered society is not Utopia, but one which is sometimes referred to as 'quasi-stable'.

The question of stability or 'quasi stability' involves the capacity of a democratic society to experience disturbance of its social institutions, which are then able to tolerate or accommodate reform before returning to a fresh equilibrium of justice. Such a society would be able to progress through evolution—rather than through revolution—and the policing of it could be 'principled'. In seeking a definition of this stability, Rawls adopts that of Harvey Leibenstein:

> A well-ordered society is quasi-stable with respect to the justice of its institutions, and the sense of justice needed to maintain this condition. Whilst a shift in social circumstances may render its institutions no longer just, in due course they are reformed as the situation requires and justice is restored.[2]

There would be no place for the laws of the Medes and the Persians in the well-ordered society, as these would be likely to render liberal democracies socially combustible. In the unstable society, police, along with other institutions, would serve to compound injustice.

Before embarking upon an examination of the events of 1968-1972, so far as they affect the policing of Northern Ireland, there are some general issues concerning the social order which I would like to address.

Historicism and the two traditions
Firstly there is what Popper called the theory of *historicism*,[3] which for those who believe in it 'gives certainty regarding the ultimate outcome of human history'. One example of historicism is the theory of the chosen people, that is people who believe that they are chosen by God as the instrument to fulfil his purpose; this is a theistic form, but there are other forms such as naturalistic, and spiritual historicism. In his valuable work *Interpreting Northern Ireland*, John Whyte records that

> Anyone who studies Northern Ireland must be struck by the intensity of feeling which the conflict evokes. It seems to go beyond what is required by a rational defence of the divergent interests which undoubtedly exist. There is an emotional element here, a welling-up of deep unconscious forces.[4]

Many nationalist supporters of insurgency in Northern Ireland do say 'history is on our side', and through this historicist view of their circumstances it is believed that victory will accrue to Catholic insurgence because that is in the nature of things, as if flowing from an historic pattern towards predictable outcomes. On the other, or Protestant side, it may equally be averred that as in the past their identity as a tribe calls for violent resistance to counter-aggression of insurgent nationalists, and so it will in the future. There seems little room left here for reason.

Historicism, Popper said, is the theory which 'expresses the feeling of being swept into the future by irresistible forces', described above by Whyte. Historicist views also lead to a ready acceptance of the false comforts of totalitarianism. Where it is believed that the dye is cast and events will take their predictable course, no room is left for reason and rationality. Popper expressed his 'frank hostility' to such ideas which 'are futile and worse, since they leave no room for a change of course to better things through reason'.[5]

Though the idea of irreversible forces of destiny may belong to superstition and lead to obstruction of social progress through reason, it is nevertheless a factor which has to be allowed for, particularly when it appears to be virulent, as it seems to be in Northern Ireland.

The social order in Northern Ireland is often described as embodying two traditions, the Catholic and the Protestant, or sometimes the Nationalist and the Unionist,[6] but it would be equally correct to speak of two tribes. Tribalism is an element found in historicist theory, as e.g. in my earlier reference to God's chosen people. Such ideas provide the strongest motivations for resisting diversion form historic destiny whilst also providing certainty in the ultimate outcome of history.[7]

Throughout this chapter we shall become aware that the concept of liberal democratic government not only failed but actually exacerbated the tribal divisions, and hostilities. Since the partition of Northern Ireland, power has resided permanently in a tribal majority which was not imbued with a public conception of justice towards the minority; whilst amongst the minority there were virulent nationalist tendencies seeking to overthrow the authority of government by force—a volatile political mixture.

The Rawlsian idea of the well-ordered society, 'designed to advance the good of its members' by a public conception of justice which 'everyone accepts and knows that others accept the same principles of justice', was not in evidence.

As we examine just four years of history, we shall become aware that step by step, and influenced by history's grip, and the lack of political will and reasoning to break with that history, there occurred a ratchet like escalation of the forces of violence.

Northern Ireland 1968

This is not the place to go into the long and at times tragic circumstances of Ango-Irish history. I propose only to consider events of the years from 1968 to 1972 in order to illustrate and to consider those matters with which we are here concerned. In particular we are to put to the test those theories of principled policing referred to in *Chapter 1*, and the Rawlsian idea of a well-ordered society based on the theory of the social contract. I believe that for our purposes these four years represent an almost coherent phase in the history of disorder in Northern Ireland, with its bitter legacy of sectarian violence and strife.

The province of Northern Ireland was largely a self-governing entity in 1968, and was certainly so in terms of law and order. The partitioning of Ireland arose out of the Anglo-Irish treaty of 1921, following which civil war took place in the new dominion of Eire as it then was, as Republican Nationalists sought to see Ireland geographically united.

During these years Northern Ireland's population consisted of approximately one-and-a half million people, two-thirds of whom were Protestants and one-third Catholics. The dichotomy was compounded by custom: 'the two factors which did most to divide Protestants as a whole from Catholics as a whole are indogamy and separate education [insisted upon by the Catholic Church]'.[3]

This disparity when drawn along sectarian and tribal lines, resulted in a permanent Protestant majority in the Northern Ireland Parliament.

Civil rights: The tinder

It is not surprising that where a significant number of people do not accept and support the same principles of justice, or where basic social institutions, such as government, education, police and others are notably lacking in justice, there is a cause for civil disobedience. In the Irish historical context this might be expected to escalate into some form of armed rebellion, but in any case violence was posited by circumstance. It is against this kind of background that the emergence of the Civil Rights Movement took place in 1967.

A Campaign for Social Justice in Northern Ireland was founded in 1964, and 'inspired in particular by resentment against what they (Catholic middle-class) regarded as sectarian bias of Unionist (Protestant) councils in the Dungannon area'.[9] The purpose of this movement was social reform, including opposition to discrimination against Catholics by local Protestant councils, particularly regarding the adult franchise in local elections, as well as fairer electoral boundaries for local government (these were subject to gerrymandering in favour of Unionists). They were not concerned, as an organization, with altering the constitutional structure of Northern Ireland, as were Nationalist movements including the IRA.[10]

There are, as with most things in the government of Northern Ireland, differences of emphasis and of degree concerning administration against Catholics, but one point of view considers that 'The fact remains that, owing to local conditions, the power of the government was used in the interests of Unionists and Protestants, with scant regard for the interests of the region as a whole, or for the claims and susceptibilities of the substantial minority'.[11]

The Northern Ireland Civil Rights Association (NICRA) modelled itself on the British National Council for Civil Liberties, and developed a very strong, mainly but not exclusively, Catholic backing and support:

> . . . it would however be a grave political and social error to regard the Civil Rights movement as narrowly sectarian or subversively political; it was and is a movement which drew, and still draws, support form a wide measure of moderate opinion on many sides, and to that extent is a moral phenomenon in the political firmament of Northern Ireland.[12]

In the beginning at least, the movement was not politically subversive or narrowly sectarian, and had the political climate been that of a 'well-ordered society', the aspirations of NICRA might have been met by redress of genuine grievance instead of injustice. Had this happened, the movement may have been less vulnerable to infiltration by activists with a political agenda of their own which included the ending of partition in Ireland, if necessary by violence. This latter element was of growing concern to the Protestants and a driving force of their Unionism.

The constitution of NICRA provided that membership was open to all people of any persuasion who agreed to abide by its objects, which were 'To assist in the maintenance of civil liberties, including freedom of speech, propaganda and assembly [this freedom became hotly disputed and was generally obstructed by the Unionists]' and to 'advance measures for the recovery and enlargement of such liberties'.

The Civil Rights Movement of the late 1960s was, according to Whyte, certainly not Unionist (Protestant). But 'since the point of its campaign was to secure British rights for British subjects it could not fairly be described as Nationalist either'.[13]

It is a matter of regret that at this time, particularly in the absence of a United Kingdom Bill of Rights—coupled with the lack of political power of the minority—the only course left open to draw attention to grievances was to take protest to the streets. Thus NICRA could march in protest and seek to exercise democratic rights, but when such measures became obstructed, sometimes violently, the association became a ready-made vehicle for Nationalist violent protest; either that or the abandonment of their purpose. It is also important to remember that under the Public Order (Northern Ireland) Act 1951, the Ulster government had wide powers to prohibit assemblies and processions, and to control opposition to processions approved by the minister.

97

Opposition to NICRA public protest became a Protestant strategy, usually on the often specious grounds that it was an IRA movement.

The powers of the Royal Ulster Constabulary are also wide. The controversial Civil Authorities (Special Powers) Act (Northern Ireland) 1922 was enacted at a time of undoubted emergency when public order in the Province had seriously deteriorated. Extreme elements in the National Republican faction sought violently to bring about the downfall of the state of Northern Ireland. As recently as the period 1956 to 1962 the Irish Republican Army had conducted a campaign of widespread shootings and explosions. The situation is clearly spelled out in the following passage:

> When the nature and powers given to the RUC [Royal Ulster Constabulary] and USC [Ulster Special Constabulary] under what is usually called the Special Powers Act are being considered or criticised, it has to be borne in mind that the Act was originally passed at a time of undoubted emergency caused by campaigns of mutual murder and reprisal from which the whole community suffered in the years 1920 and 1921, that the Irish Republican Army continued a campaign of violence as recently as the period between 1956 and 1962, and there is evidence that its objectives remain the same even if temporarily its tactics vary.[14]

Whatever the position may have been in 1920, since the promulgation of the Universal Declaration of Human Rights in 1948, this Act has been in conflict with those articles concerning arbitrary arrest, the presumption of innocence, personal privacy, and freedom of opinion and expression. NICRA was soon to exploit, to stress, and to campaign against these and other allegations of injustice.

All these shortcomings and a failure of government to investigate and to remedy complaints caused much frustration and resentment. There was particularly strong resentment among Catholics regarding the nature and existence of the Ulster Special Constabulary as a partisan para-military force recruited exclusively form Protestants, and to the Special Powers Act, which gave the police their very wide powers. Meanwhile fears amongst the majority of Protestants of an increasing Catholic populace, with its political implications, and the history of IRA violence, only heightened the tensions and raised the threshold of civil war.

Earlier I examined the question of civil disobedience (see p. 96), and it is timely to remind ourselves of what Rawls has to say on the use of the police apparatus to maintain control in a society which is not 'well-ordered':

> *. . . if justified civil disobedience seems to threaten civic concord, the responsibility falls not upon those who protest, but upon those whose abuse of authority and power justifies such opposition. For to employ the coercive apparatus of the state in order to maintain manifestly unjust institutions is itself a form of illegitimate force that men in due course have a right to resist.* [15] (Emphasis supplied).

The expression 'to resist' means 'to disobey', but not to be violent in this context.

In 1968 many of the Catholic minority of Northern Ireland appeared to have reached a stage where, in the absence of legitimate political power and influence, protest was the only way to seek a remedy for injustices. Unfortunately there was a widespread lack of respect amongst the Protestant majority for the right of the minority to protest, and regrettably the IRA were preparing in the wings.

The example of Martin Luther King's Civil Rights Movement in the USA at this time provided stimulus for protest movements generally. In many ways the position of the Catholic Community in Northern Ireland bore similar injustice to that of the black community in the southern states of the USA. It is ironic that in both cases what began as a non-violent and morally justified campaign of civil disobedience became a campaign of violence when adopted by extremists.

The young Gerry Adams, later to be leader of the Sinn Fein Republican political party (front organisation for the IRA) recalls watching the black civil rights movement in the USA and wrote:

> [It] not only had its obvious influence in terms of the anthem *We Shall Overcome* but also in terms of its affinity within the six counties [Ulster]. Courtesy of television we were able to see an example of the fact that you don't just have to take it. You could fight back, you could fight back. [16]

But whereas the black civil rights movement in the USA could petition the Supreme Court under its Constitutional Bill of Rights, which it did successfully against segregation and other denials of rights, there was no equivalent route to redress of grievance in the UK.

The IRA
At this time the Irish Republican Army (IRA) having failed in its campaign of violence from 1956 to 1962 to bring about the fusion between Northern Ireland and the Irish Republic, had to some extent abandoned 'war' in favour of protest and civil disobedience. The organization sustained a schism between what were called its Official arm (political) and the Provisionals (violent). The former mixed its traditional Republicanism with non-sectarianism and Marxist tendencies

99

for its political base. Tactics were based on the Campaign for Nuclear Disarmament in Britain. It is alleged that this strategy of the IRA was 'an attitude that ended up paralysing them when sectarian violence in the North broke out in the Autumn of 1968'.[17]

The evidence seems to support the view that in 1968 the IRA was not ready for another campaign, and official reports were explicit on this. In his book *Pig in the Middle*, Desmond Hamill, an experienced reporter and author quotes a Special Branch report which said that

> the speed of success of the [Civil Rights Association] in producing the present condition in the streets has caught the IRA largely unprepared in the military sense . . . and reliable sources report a shortage of arms.

A New Scotland Yard report stated that

> The Northern Ireland Civil Rights Association is at first a genuinely broad based organization [this was also the view of the Cameron Commission]. The IRA . . . is not organized or equipped to play a significant independent role within this body.[18]

Although the Republican Movement was busily joining the NICRA, militarily the IRA was unprepared, whilst at the same time the Unionist majority manifested anxiety. Fearing a threat to their dominance and to their very identity as a community, extremists from the Unionist majority sought to obstruct NICRA's protest at every opportunity, often through blatantly illegal or unfair tactics. NICRA's leaders realising they were attracting attention and support from political extremists condemned such infiltration but the tide was beginning to turn.

Unionist reactions to the civil rights protest were fuelled by inaccurate perceptions of attitudes in the Catholic community. Whyte was of the view that had data now available concerning Catholic attitudes been available in 1967, more Protestants might have been reassured and thérefore more willing to compromise.[19]

Londonderry 5 October 1968: the ratchet begins
On 5 October 1968, NICRA, together with Londonderry activists, proposed a march to take place in the city in order to exercise their rights of protest against their civic condition entailing the numerous injustices referred to earlier. These injustices were catalogued with great clarity in the Cameron Report in the judgment of which they were to be seriously regarded in any analysis of the immediate causes of the disturbances. And 'very many people of all shades of political opinion recognised the case and need for redress and reform'.[20]

The route proposed by NICRA for their march was bound to be provocative to the Protestant residents as it followed their own historic route. In accordance with legal requirements an application was submitted to the minister of home affairs for approval of the march. The view has been expressed that 'the civil rights marchers wanted to process from the Protestant side to the Catholic side to symbolise their non-sectarian basis'.[21]

The immediate response of their Protestant opponents was to complain that the Republican character of the march was an affront to their historic traditions, and they threatened a counter demonstration. In addition another Protestant organization applied to the minister for permission to march over the same route on the same day; this undoubtedly was a disingenuous ploy to have the NICRA march banned, and in this it succeeded.

The banning of the NICRA march by the minister was supported by the police and this created an impression of bias towards the Protestant cause—and later the police were criticised by the Cameron Inquiry for mistaken judgment. The decision to ban the march 'placed upon the police an impossible strain and burden' and was 'mischievous'.

The ban was regarded by the Catholic community as unjust. At a meeting called by the organizers, a number of more militant people managed to force through a vote that the march should go ahead in defiance of the ban. In the words of the subsequent inquiry the minister's prohibition was

> to transform the situation. It guaranteed the attendance of a large number of citizens of Londonderry who actively resented what appeared to them to be totally unwarranted interference by the minister.[22]

Resulting from the inability of the police, and some of the organizers, peacefully to control the protest, the wilder elements amongst the marchers pelted the police with various missiles, and the police made baton charges on marchers trapped without an escape route. By now the protest march was as unlawful as that of Martin Luther King in Birmingham, Alabama, in 1964. The police charges on the crowd were later described by the Cameron Inquiry as 'indiscriminately' made. Water-cannon were turned on the crowds of people including merely passive onlookers and further violence followed police seizure of banners carried by some of the marchers. Disorder escalated and rioting continued throughout the night and during the following day. Police strength was inadequate, reflecting inefficient planning and the police failure to dominate or control events led to rioting for several days. Eleven police officers and 77 civilians sustained injury.[23]

National and international news media reports of events in Londonderry at this time ensured some very damaging pictures of police violence which caused anger and concern. This resulted in the widespread formation of protest movements, including the People's Democracy based at Queen's University, Belfast. Founded on legal and peaceful objectives this movement over the next few years was to participate in many conflicts with the police.

Meanwhile the IRA strategy remained: '. . . to provoke the police into over-reaction and thus spark off mass reaction against the authorities'.[24]

The purposes of the IRA strategy were of the kind which high police should seek to deny. To allow the police to over-react is both incompetent and unwise in policing terms. It is just as possible to win over the situation by appearing to lose, as it is to lose although appearing to win, as we shall see. In these matters there is a dimension of public 'hearts and minds', and in tense situations winning the hearts and minds can be more important than enforcing the laws.

The task of the police is to keep the peace, but this is a concept which is not conterminous with the concept of legality. Law enforcement is of course part of the concept of keeping the peace, though it is not the only part. If, in order to enforce laws, methods are used which in themselves result in the spread of disorder, then the peace has been disproportionately broken, and should widespread social damage arise therefrom it could be said that the remedy is worse than the disease. Compromise has its place when policing the people's peace is being considered, unlike the philosophy of war of which it has been said that '. . . to introduce into the philosophy of war itself a principle of moderation would be an absurdity' for 'war is an act of violence pushed to its utmost bounds'[25] which policing most certainly is not.

Major General Richard Clutterbuck commenting on the events of October 5 was of the view

that the radical element was to override the civil rights leadership and press home the confrontation, to which the RUC reacted somewhat roughly, setting in motion the train of events which within four years was to kill so many people.[26]

The Cameron inquiries

Following the disorderly and violent events in Londonderry on 5 October 1968, the governor of Northern Ireland appointed an inquiry under Lord Cameron's experienced leadership.[27] The inquiry reported

that [evidence of] social and economic grievances, or abuses of political power [were] such that we felt compelled to conclude that they had substantial foundation in fact, and were in a very real sense an immediate and operative cause of the demonstration and subsequent disorders after 5 October 1968.

The social, economic and political failures were sufficiently marked to render Northern Ireland a not well-ordered society in the Rawlsian sense. Thus it was that however much the policing of the minority population was regarded as unjust, the underlying cause was a political one.

The police action in Londonderry on 5 October 1968 drew the following comment from the Cameron inquiry:

> In the majority of cases we find that the police acted with commendable discipline and restraint under very great strain and provocation from various quarters. [29]

The inquiry was to record however a deterioration in police behaviour through unnecessary violence towards Roman Catholic demonstrators, and they 'record with regret' the serious misconduct of police officers who attacked, assaulted, and damaged the property of innocent people in the Bogside [Catholic] area of Londonderry. The effect of this was 'rousing passions and inspiring hostility towards the police', which was 'regrettably great'. There was no doubt on the evidence that police conduct was *'an immediate and contributing cause of the disorders which subsequently occurred'.*[29] (Emphasis supplied).

There are lessons to be learned by police commanders and junior officers from an examination of these events. From this time forward the police were gradually to withdraw patrols form the Bogside area, named by its defenders 'Free Derry'. The Army prudently kept a lower profile save for the occasional patrol in strength behind the barricades which the IRA had organized.

Where the forces of law and order are prevented from entering a district without full scale violent conflict this is a clear indication of a breakdown in the social order.

The Cameron Inquiry did note that the police were not always adequate for the difficult task they had to perform. But to the Civil Rights Movement the policing inadequacy appeared to them to be a reluctance to protect them from Protestant ambushers and violence. There was a special hatred by the Catholics towards the Ulster Special Constabulary which emerged as a biased sectarian force, wholly Protestant, and unable or unwilling to act impartially as police in a democracy should.

The virus spreads

Throughout 1969 the social order of this 'not well-ordered' province was to experience violence and counter-violence of an extreme kind as sections of the two tribes vented their anger and their fears upon each other. During the Spring and Summer a series of incidents involving riot and near anarchy throughout the Province was to overwhelm the resources of the police and thereby the system of criminal justice.

The People's Democracy march from Belfast to Londonderry on January 1 to 4 was organized by a rump of the main committee, and though peacefully intended it was certain to provoke, and was duly ambushed by Protestant opponents at Burntollet Bridge on the approaches to Londonderry. The marchers were violently attacked suffering substantial casualties, and the episode once more highlighted the failure of the police to protect lawful demonstrators of the minority, and so the Rule of Law once more was overborne, and the moderate civil rights activists were outflanked by the more extreme.

The Northern Ireland government now began to offer reforms to the Catholic population which had been peacefully requested in recent times, but it seems that events were beginning to conspire against peaceful change. There was some doubt as to when the reforms would be implemented and the offer came late and perhaps too late as a momentum of anger had developed. Even more sinister was the Protestant backlash towards the proposed change.

> On the last day of March and during the month of April [1969] there occurred a number of explosions at electricity and water installations in the province . . . they were the work of Protestant extremists who were anxious to undermine confidence in the government of Captain O'Neil, prime minister. At the time it was widely thought that the explosions were the work of the IRA, though it is quite clear now that they were not. [30]

Sections of the Protestant community poured scourn on Captain O'Neil's attempts to meet the demands of NICRA, and as they withdrew support from their own government the prime minister had little option but to resign—once the Rawlsian principles of a well-ordered society were denied.

Acts of violence and civil disturbance reached a crescendo in August when the most severe internecine violence between Protestants and Catholics took place in the cities of Londonderry and Belfast and other towns and places throughout the Province. The loss of life, personal injury, and damage to houses and other buildings, including chapels and churches set on fire, pesented a civil war scenario based on historical tribal and religious divisions.

Eight Catholics and two Protestants were shot and killed; 87 Catholics and 61 Protestants were shot; and 203 Catholics and 170 Protestants were injured. Many families were rendered homeless as their houses were set on fire, this mainly by Protestants.[31]

Military Aid

Police resources were now stretched beyond their limits and at 4.30 a.m on 15 August 1969, the Inspector General of the Royal Ulster Constabulary requested of the Northern Ireland government ministers and the government of the United Kingdom that the British Army should now be deployed in aid of the civil power to maintain order in a rapidly deteriorating situation.

Lord Scarman was of the view that invocation of military aid 'creates as many problems as it solves'.[32] Whilst law and order in the Province was the responsibility of the Northern Ireland government, the operational control of the Army always remained with the UK government, a constitutional situation giving rise to difficult problems of accountability. There were inevitably political problems in so far as to seek military aid was a tacit admission that the Northern Ireland government was no longer able to govern.

In a sense it is imposing on soldiers to cast them in the role of police officers, since their training is to prepare them for war or its prevention. As the United Kingdom, unlike France, has no quasi-military bodies such as the Gendarmerie, when the police are overwhelmed, British soldiers are required to significantly change their role. The nature of policing with all its nuances, and shades of accountability and legality amongst the civil population, is quite distinct from the role of the soldier defending his country against the armies of external powers.

It is true that as the civil violence escalates into terrorist campaigns the skills of soldiers come into their own, but in August 1969 the priority for policing the 'peoples peace' meant standing between the tribal factions, protecting the innocent, and preventing serious crimes of a public nature. The British Army's wide colonial experience was without doubt an advantage at times, whilst at others it might have been a disadvantage. Such arrangements only buy time, and, as Scarman commented, '. . . it is a reasonable inference that their role was expected to be very limited'.[33]

As things turned out the British Army was soon to play the primary role in the maintaining of public order for far longer than anyone envisaged.

In his evidence to the Scarman inquiry, Brigadier Hudson of the British Army said that

> the military were ready to come to the aid of the civil power when the circumstances are such that the civil power, whatever its resources, reckons that if they get any worse they are going to lose control. In other words, not after they have lost control, but when they are about to . . .

The request for military aid had been couched in terms of an imminent risk of IRA infiltration from the Republic of Ireland, but the subsequent inquiry found no proof of this. The appreciation of the situation by the police that they

> had on their hands an armed uprising led by the IRA was incorrect . . . there is no credible evidence that the IRA planned or organized the disturbances.[34]

Troops were soon deployed on the streets of Belfast where a semblance of order was gradually restored, and the British Army began its long, challenging and arduous task of maintaining order, and together with the RUC mounting anti-insurgency operations; they were to sustain many casualties in pursuit of their role. This period is of particular interest as the military GOC was designated the 'director of peace keeping operations', establishing the primacy of the army. Within six months of embarking upon their function, some 55 people had been killed and 600 treated for wounds and injuries in violence and counter-violence.

SCARMAN INQUIRES

On 27 August 1969, both Houses of Parliament in Northern Ireland passed a resolution to the governor to appoint another tribunal of inquiry. The highly respected British judge, Lord Scarman, was appointed to inquire into a 'definite matter of urgent public importance, that is to say the acts of violence and civil disturbance' which had recently occurred.

Scarman made no bones about the purpose of his inquiry: 'It was', he said, 'an investigation of police conduct'. He utterly rejected the suggestion that generally it was a case 'of a partisan force co-operating with Protestant mobs to attack Catholic people'. This, he said, 'was devoid of substance'.[35] He quoted the readiness of the police to do their duty against Protestant mobs during the Belfast riots of 2 to 4 August 1969. During these riots Scarman found that 'the Protestants were those ready to provoke trouble; the Catholics were looking only to their defence'.

During this desperate time 'police behaviour and tactics were exemplary' and 'They did their utmost to protect the lives and property of all sections of the community' and largely succeeded, and 'they dealt firmly and efficiently with law breakers, who in this case were Protestants'.[36]

The fateful split

By July 1969 it was 'painfully clear' that the 'Catholic minority no longer believed that the RUC was impartial, and that the Catholics and civil rights activists were publicly asserting this loss of confidence'. This hostility meant that the police came to treat their critics as their enemies and also the enemies of the public peace. 'Thus there developed a fateful split between the Catholic community and the police'.[37] Distrusted by a substantial section of the whole population, and short of numbers, the RUC had by now lost the capacity to control major disturbances.

Scarman sets out six occasions on which the police had been seriously at fault in their handling of the disturbances of August 1969. He found that the police acted as if they were faced with an armed uprising engineered by the IRA, and this belief encouraged loss of usual constraint by the police. In this they were mistaken for 'there is no credible evidence that the IRA planned or organized the disturbances'.[38]

By concentrating his enquiry on the police, Scarman was able to show that the High Police continued to act throughout as though they had adequate resources. This was a serious miscalculation. Scarman praised the rank and file police officers for their courage, 'which under appalling circumstances was beyond praise', and to record that their ultimate failure to maintain order at this time was due to sheer exhaustion and shortage of numbers. Scarman then went on to make what in the author's view is one of the classic statements concerning politics and policing, deserving the most careful consideration:

> Once large-scale communal disturbances occur they are not susceptible to control by the police. Either they must be suppressed by overwhelming force, which save in the last resort, is not acceptable in our society, and was not within the control of the NI government; or a political solution must be devised. There are limits to the efficiency of the police and the criminal law; confronted with such disturbances the police and ordinary processes of the criminal law are of no avail.[39]

By this time prospects for 'principled policing' even had they existed, had evaporated, since the underlying nature of the political and social chaos prevented any such prospect. The state of public order continued to deteriorate.

Non-violent protests of the Civil Rights Association had gradually been forced to give way, and the Provisional IRA were now on the offensive, better organized and ruthless. The Army found itself being sucked into a morass of internecine conflict, a Catholic backlash against Protestant violence, during which time the Army shot and killed its first two gunmen. The Home Affairs minister at the time spoke in defence of the army now gradually being alienated from the Catholics. The minister said 'he believed that it may be necessary to shoot even more'. The sectarian conflict over such things as marching and counter-marching of the factions continued to increase the tension.

In its desperation to bring public disorder and violence in the Province under control, the NI government began to turn its attention to the extreme measure of internment without trial. The ratchet-like turn of events had not yet finished its damaging course.

INTERNMENT—'A HIGH RISK POLICY'

It is general experience in these matters that the introduction of internment without trial is so exceptional a measure that if not handled with clinical precision its whole purpose will be defeated. In a 'well-ordered' society it only has its place as an ultimate short-term expedient for government to carry out its contractual duties of the protection of the lives of citizens, but most certainly not for sectarian party political purposes whatsoever.

Within a state which is convulsed by violence 'threatening the life of the nation', e.g. widespread terrorism, extraordinary measures may be taken by governments, e.g. preventive custody of suspected terrorists and active supporters, when there is some evidence to support such a course, but not just arbitrarily.[40] A law justifying these exceptional measures must comply with the Rule of Law (see p. 33).

Sympathy for untried internees may soon build up, and may be reflected in international opinion. An efficient, honest propaganda is desirable if the government case is legally and ethically correct.

A falsely imprisoned person is not without remedy at common law; it would be lawful and moral to escape (self-help remedy), to seek a writ of *habeas corpus*, or to sue for damages. In the Northern Ireland case the 'hunger strike' and reversion to filth and squalor by internees in defiance of prison rules were forms of drawing attention to their predicament.

Effective policing requires that police and soldiers, when engaged on policing activities, have adequate powers to achieve the goals set for them. When we considered the Rule of Law it was pointed out that the rule did not necessarily serve justice, or indeed principled policing, though that may be its ultimate intention. In times of civil war, terrorist campaigns and war itself, governments of liberal democracies invariably enact statutes which increase police powers, and suspend some civil liberties, e.g. freedom of speech, and of association. In 1922 the Northern Ireland Parliament had passed the Civil Authorities (Special Powers) Act (Northern Ireland) which provided sweeping powers unknown in 'peace' time. This Act, amongst other things, gives power to the secretary of state to order the internment without trial of people suspected of belonging to certain terrorist or para-military organizations and being engaged in activities to violently and unlawfully usurp the government.

Although internment without trial is *prima facie* a contravention of article 5 of the European Convention on Human Rights and Fundamental Freedoms, there is provision that in time of war or other public emergency threatening the life of the nation, a government may suspend or derogate therefrom. Once again this raised constitutional conundrums, since the government of the United Kingdom, being the signatory or Contracting Party to the Convention would have to seek derogation from article 5, therefore the United Kingdom's agreement to internment without trial was sought by the NI government; after much hesitation and debate this was granted. The first and controversial and political hurdle had been cleared, and now all attention turned to the operation itself.

At this time the British Army was the major resource for the maintenance of public order and anti-insurgent operations. It would fall to the army's lot to carry out the government's intentions. But critical to any chance of success was accurate and up-to-date intelligence concerning leading IRA terrorists. The army had little reliable intelligence of its own due to its fairly recent commitment to the task, and therefore had to rely on the intelligence records of the Royal Ulster Constabulary, which proved to be woefully inadequate. The omens were bad, and of impending disaster, placing the army in an impossible position at the outset. There were serious reservations in the higher military echelons as well as amongst the junior commanders as they were to embark on a mission for which they were not adequately informed.

The operation entitled 'Demetrius' began at 4.30 a.m. on 9 August 1971. British troops swooped on houses throughout the Province, but only houses occupied by Catholics, a fact which was to anger nationalist sentiments. Some 342 people were arrested as suspects of participation in IRA activities. That the operation was little short of a disaster soon became obvious. Of the 342 men arrested, 116 were cleared within 48 hours, and of the remainder 'no more than 80 had anything to do with the IRA', and only four were senior officers (none of them top men).[41] A senior British Army officer was quoted as saying that the operation 'was carried out at the wrong moment in the wrong way for the wrong reasons. But that wasn't much help. You've got to get the right people but instead they arrested the people who weren't really important'.[42] The views of a senior cabinet minister in British government, William Whitelaw, later to become minister for Northern Ireland under direct British rule, expressed his view that

> Internment without trial is, to risk the obvious, a serious decision which can be justified only if it succeeds in reducing violence [Operation Demetrius as it was called ignited a wave of violence and condemnation, a price from which there was to be no recovery: author's note]. It must, however, be accepted that before it can succeed it is bound to increase tension, and so initially for this reason it is a high risk policy.[43]

William Whitelaw went on to stress the absolute necessity for accurate intelligence and he believed that too many people were detained a 'large proportion' of whom were not really terrorists at all.

An independent view from an experienced writer and author of a definitive account of the army's role, Desmond Hamill, was that

> Beyond doubt the real error lay once again in the inability to realise that an insurgency campaign is a war for people's minds. Internment was totally one-sided. No Protestants were arrested and it was certainly not because Protestant's hands were clean from terrorism. It was resentment over this and over what the Catholics saw as the brutality of the soldiers, that fuelled the orgy of destruction and pushed the communities ever further into their bitter enclaves.[44]

Within 36 hours 17 people were killed and hundreds of houses destroyed. Buses and cars were hijacked and incinerated, police attacked with stones and petrol bombs, the army came under fire and volunteers to the IRA flooded in. Regarding Operation Demetrius as a victory for them, the IRA proclaimed 'This is war'.[45] In the following five months 97 people were killed. If this was a disaster for the government it was certainly a negation of all that represents a well-ordered society. There now followed further legal and moral issues to be faced by the government of the United Kingdom.

Complaints of torture and inhuman and degrading treatment of internees were preferred by the government of the Republic of Ireland to the European Commission on Human Rights. In the even the UK government was cleared of the torture allegation, though a majority of the Court of Human Rights found them guilty of inhuman and degrading treatment.

Some junior commanders were disillusioned by the role of the British Army in enforcing the policy of internment without trial. Writing in the *Royal Marine Regimental Magazine* at the time, 45 Commando frankly expressed a common, though politically embarrassing, view:

> The British Army, as the instrument of internment, has become the object of Catholic animosity. Since that day the street battles, countless explosions, migration from mixed areas and cold-blooded killings have done little to reassure us that internment would, by the removal of the gunner provide a return to a semblance of law and order, a basis for a political solution to Ulster's problems. Ironically, it appears to have produced the opposite effect. [46]

Internment, it was said, had strengthened the IRA, alienated the Catholic population, and made the prospects for civic accord even more remote. That this outcome seems not to have been anticipated by the NI and UK governments was unsettling and demoralising; political leadership appeared to have failed.

The general officer commanding, General Sir Harry Tuzo, was reported as having said some time later that 'internment was not an instantaneous [sic] success, and that the error was perhaps that we were too undiscriminating . . . that is where we slipped up'.[47] It was indeed a slip-up and one exacting a heavy price. By the end of 1971, 43 soldiers had been killed, and the year 1972 began not with a more pacified populace, but one within which violence and bloodshed proved to be shocking beyond all expectations. At this stage no-one seems to have been able to devise strategies, either political or police, for reducing conflict.

Political consequences of the introduction of internment without trial were dire. The Catholic community and its leaders were in open rebellion against the NI government. Councillors and MPs withdrew from participation with the Stormont Parliament and local government councils. One leading advocate of non-violent democratic reform and a Stormont MP, John Hulme, expressed views which go to the very core of the theory of 'quasi-stability' as earlier described:

> . . . we do not recognise the authority of the Stormont Parliament . . . and we do not care twopence whether this is treason or not. Ever since then [1921] we have had government without consensus, because the full consensus of all the people has not been given to the system of government, and when you have a situation like that, you have *a situation of permanent instability* [emphasis supplied], and when you have a permanent instability

you have recurring acts of violence and surely that has been the history of the 50 years of this system of government.[48]

In this way the police and the army, being arms of government, no longer had credibility among the Catholic one-third of the populace; their *de facto* legitimacy did not exist; they were enemies, and therefore targets for the IRA, and at times even of extreme Protestant military groups. As if to underline this state of revolt, statistics of dead and injured began to rise. Within four months of internment, 30 soldiers, eleven police and auxiliaries and 73 civilians had been killed. By the middle of December 1971, 1,576 people had been interned, 934 released, leaving over 600 still interned without trial.

By now the army rightly viewed the main threat to be IRA terrorists, and in turn they themselves were viewed by the nationalists as the enemy. The denouement of our inquiry was now approaching.

At this time all parades and marches were banned throughout the Province by government decree, but the Catholic activists, just like Martin Luther King, had developed a sense of moral rectitude which transcended their commitment to constitutional legality. At times the state was ungovernable.

LONDONDERRY, SUNDAY 30 JANUARY 1972

The NICRA planned an anti-internment march and protest to take place in Londonderry on Sunday, 30 January 1972. Catholic enclaves in Londonderry were no longer susceptible to routine policing by the RUC. These strongholds of nationalist and anti-government protests were protected by barricades manned by vigilantes. The Bogside was now labelled 'Free Derry' by its Republican defenders. Only the army had the means to enter the territory with confidence for by now The Bogside had its own army in the form of the IRA. The situation was very reminiscent of that which faced the French authorities in Algiers in the late 1950s when French Paratroop Regiments were assigned for duty in the Casbah Arab quarter with its terrorist FLN, as casualties among police patrols became unacceptable.

The bane of both police and soldiers in Londonderry were well organized gangs of unemployed young Catholic men described as 'hooligans', who acted as a scourge to the authorities by arson and violence to property, and in violence through missile throwing— including home made petrol and nail bombs—at both police and military. Soldiers and police became very wary of these hooligans who were able to evade identification and arrest through their fleetness of foot and knowledge of the alley-ways and footpaths. It would have served the purposes of both army and police to have them subject to effective law enforcement, and it was part of the Army s strategy to bring this about which led to such a deadly outcome on this Sunday of NICRA's march.

NICRA's route

Lord Widgery in his Tribunal report on these events stated as his conclusion number 1, that 'there would have been no deaths in Londonderry on January 30 if those who organized the illegal march had not thereby created a highly dangerous situation in which a clash between demonstrators and the security forces was almost inevitable'.[49] For our purposes we would have to accept the logic of that comment, but it fails to say that had there been no abuse of internment there would have been no march. This situation raises once more the important question of the lack of a Bill of Rights under which UK citizens may seek redress of grievances against the government in judicial proceedings rather than through sometimes provocative public parades and the news media's reportage of scenes of disorder.

NICRA planned the march to start in the Catholic Creggan area and thence to march to the city centre, regarded as Protestant territory, to hold a public meeting outside the Londonderry Guildhall. After due consideration the army high command, following consultation with the police, decided to let the march take place and that although it was illegal it may well be peaceful. The march however was to be confined to the Catholic area, and barricades were erected to achieve this. Here we see discretion being used not to enforce laws when doing so would be likely to lead to a riotous and dangerous situation.

'Scooping up' the hooligans

Anticipating the presence of their *bête noir*, the hooligan youth, with their taunts and missiles, army plans were prepared for mass arrests to take place when the hooligans began their usual missile attacks and thereby became separated from the rest of the march.

There appears to have been no doubt that the army commanders planned for an unusually high strength of troops on the ground supported by armoured vehicles. Furthermore the troops were to include a battalion of seasoned paratroops with plenty of active peace-keeping service behind them in the sectarian ghettos of Belfast, where they were regarded with some trepidation by the disorderly youth. If the hooligans wanted a fight, as they often did, they were to meet a determined and professional foe. Young paratroopers cannot be expected to comport themselves with the mien and gravitas of the patrolling police officer in less violent times. They were facing a degree of civil war, and in war the

113

rules may be regarded differently. During guerrilla warfare moralities are terribly confused. To help the soldiers through this dilemma they were issued with 'Yellow Cards' containing standing orders about the use of firearms which Widgery regarded as 'satisfactory'.

It is a matter of interest that Londonderry's senior police officer, Superintendent Frank Lagan of the RUC, himself a Catholic, favoured a more conciliatory posture towards banning the march outside the Catholic area. Using his discretion he would have allowed it to go ahead to avoid violence, prosecuting photographed leaders at a later date. As it happened though the march was stopped from leaving the Catholic ghetto, it offered no violence, and Widgery concluded that the army strategy was successful so far; he was less certain about the decision to make mass arrests of hooligans.

The NICRA march set off gathering some 5,000 followers as it went, though by the time it concluded only some 500 stayed behind to listen to speeches; the whole was an orderly affair. About this time a single rifle shot was heard to strike a drainpipe on the Presbyterian Church. The shot was believed to have come from a nearby tower block housing a sniper.

As had been anticipated the 'Derry Young Hooligans' broke away from the parade and from behind a barricade began throwing missiles at the advancing soldiers. Units of the Parachute Regiment were ordered to carry out mass arrests as planned in their 'scoop-up' operation. Soon afterwards other shots were heard coming from nearby buildings and soldiers fired 32 shots in reply. No soldiers were wounded, but one 17 year old youth was killed; Widgery found he had been killed by mistake.

Soldiers now unleashed more fire power making 108 single shots in all, believing themselves to have been fired upon whilst making arrests. This shooting by the military resulted in 13 civilian males being killed, six of whom were 17 years of age, and 13 people including one woman, were wounded. The fact that this encounter was so one-sided was explained by Widgery as being due to superior training and no doubt superior equipment of the soldiers. Widgery also found that

> None of the deceased or wounded is proved to have been shot whilst handling a firearm or bomb. Some are wholly acquitted of complicity in such action; but there is a strong suspicion that some others had been firing weapons or handling bombs in the course of the afternoon and that yet others had been closely supporting them.[50]

As for the conduct of the soldiers: 'at one end of the scale some soldiers showed a high degree of responsibility; at the other . . . firing bordered on the reckless'.[51]

114

The key question in all this was whether it was a prudent decision to seek to make mass arrests of hooligans. Widgery was of the view that the day might otherwise have passed off without serious incident and he speculated that

> ... an arrest operation carried out in battalion strength in circumstances in which the troops were likely to come under fire involved hazard to civilians in the area which Commander 8 Brigade may have underestimated.[52]

These comments deserve the best attention of the high strategists of both military and police.

As news of events in Londonderry on Sunday 30 January 1972 filtered out to the world's news media it became clear that a high price was being exacted as a result. Riotous mobs attacked the British Embassy in Dublin burning it to the ground; members of the Irish diaspora supplied weapons and money and even recruits to the IRA, as did people such as Libya's dictator Gadaffi.

The conflict in Northern Ireland had grown ratchet-like in a short period of four years from a peaceful protest movement in 1968, into the beginnings of Europe's most savage terrorist campaign, costly in lives and destruction of property.

CONCLUSIONS

We are now in a position to consider the question posed at the outset, namely what are the implications for the policing function in a social order which in the Rawlsian sense is not 'well ordered'? In particular we are concerned, not just with any form of policing, but with principled policing as put forward in *Chapter 1*; namely the social contract, protectionism and the common good.

That Northern Ireland society was not well ordered is clearly highlighted in the words of John Hulme, the Social Democrat and Labour Party Member of the NI Parliament (see page 111) when speaking to the Dungiven Assembly in 1971. Castigating the system of government as being without consensus and thereby being permanently unstable, and in consequence plagued with violence he touched upon the truth. It was a society certainly not effectively regulated by a public conception of justice in which everyone accepts and knows that others accept the same principles of justice.

Had this been a well ordered society it is reasonable to believe that the Northern Ireland Civil Rights Association's peaceful campaign for better social justice for the Catholic minority would have attracted more understanding and willingness by the majority power to redress legitimate and moral grievances. Had justice responded, the subsequent disaster may not have occurred, or if it had occurred it might have been less severe.

The nature of Northern Ireland's politics at this time provided a classic example of the 'tyranny of the majority' as contemplated in the nineteenth century political thoughts of John Stuart Mill in his essay *On Liberty*. Describing democracy as being the will and power of the 'people', Mill comments that in practice it means 'the will of the most *active part*—the majority', and this majority '*may* desire to oppress part of their number, and precautions are as much needed against this as against any other abuse of power'. (emphasis supplied)[53]

Abuse of power by governments is in most systems controlled by means of written constitutions and Bills of Rights. The United Kingdom, and hence Northern Ireland, are lacking in this form of precaution. Since the advent of the United Nations with its Universal Declaration of Human Rights there is a growing awareness of the need for international sources of justice. The European Convention on Human Rights and Fundamental Freedoms was the international charter, under article 3 of which the government of the Republic of Ireland sought redress for the United Kingdom's alleged responsibility for the abuses committed by the RUC and the army interrogation units on detainees during internment without trial. It was decided that the UK security forces had practised 'inhuman and degrading treatment' of internees.[54]

It is concluded that principled policing is not possible in a society lacking in political stability as Northern Ireland was during these four years, for in the words of Lord Scarman:

> There are limits to the efficiency of the police and the criminal law: confronted with such disturbances the police and the ordinary processes of the criminal law are of no avail.

POSTSCRIPT

Sir Arthur Young (formerly Commissioner of the City of London Police) my colleague and friend visited me on 18 March 1974 at Police Headquarters at Exeter. Young was the first Englishman to be appointed Chief Constable of Northern Ireland in order to implement the police reforms resulting from Lord Hunt's Report on the Royal Ulster Constabulary in 1969.[55]

He asked to have a recorded discussion with myself and senior colleagues. The following are extracts from the transcript. Having spoken of his experiences as the senior police officer to military generals in the Gold Coast (now Ghana), Malaysia and Kenya during periods of insurgency, he went on:

I come to more recent times now because in September 1969 I was asked on a Saturday afternoon to go and see Mr. Callaghan, who was then home secretary at the Labour Party Conference in Brighton. I naturally said "What does he want to see me about?", and I was told he wanted my advice about Northern Ireland. So I went to see him and he gave me a long, as the diplomats would say, *tour dans le ronde.* He explained the situation in Northern Ireland, which I could have read through myself from the papers, and then he quite astounded me by saying he wanted me to go there. I really was astounded because I first said that I thought I was unsuitable, I thought I was too old at 62, and I thought there were a number of people more qualified. He said "Who are they" and I quickly gave him the names of my best friends!

He said "No, I want you to go and if you will accept it as a matter of duty". I said "Then I must, but what I must tell you before we go any further at all is that I think you made a grievous fundamental error in putting the police under the command of the army".

And he said "I take your point. Well if you can change it so much the better, but I must leave it to you". I said "I cannot accept otherwise".

I was forced upon the government in Stormont and the RUC by Callaghan himself. They were made to swallow this in the way they were made to swallow the recommendations of the Hunt Commission, and naturally the RUC and Stormont were not at all anxious first of all to sack their own Commissioner and to employ instead an Englishman who, if he wasn't an enemy was certainly an alien . . . It was rather like the Metropolitan Police having a Japanese general for their commissioner, as I discovered afterwards!

I think that the greatest change that took place since 1969 in Northern Ireland — because all the things that happened then had happened before, was that television was looking over the wall. The world was saying to both sides you can't do this any longer. And there were many occasions in my time when we had ten countries represented independently with their television crews to see what was going on.

At the time of my arrival there had been several rather serious riots but to look and see what has happened in the Catholic area do remember the British Army was called into Northern Ireland for the main purpose of

117

protecting the Catholics against Protestants. Even now one can look into part of The Falls area of Belfast, these awful ghettos, and find several hundred houses which had been occupied by the Catholics which had been burnt out by the rampaging Protestant mobs. I am not going to say that the powers that be, the RUC, because that's all there was, the RUC, and the "B" Specials couldn't or wouldn't—but the fact is they didn't prevent this kind of thing happening.

Even the first night I was there the rampaging mob demonstrated (they were Protestants from Shankhill Road) on behalf of the RUC . . . quite spontaneously they set off to revenge the RUC. They said, what we are going to do is to burn out the community flats. The community flats were occupied by several hundred Catholic families and it was no idle threat because the same gang had burnt out these houses before, and so they set off demonstrating on behalf of the RUC to burn out the Catholic flats.

They were met in Springfield Road by a cordon of RUC stretched across the road, who said "Stop", and without more ado they shot down three policemen on whose behalf they were demonstrating!

The difficulty with Northern Ireland at that time was that really nobody was in charge. There was no Supremo—just think of the political situation. Dennis Healey was the Secretary for Defence and therefore in command of the British Army politically. Callaghan was the home secretary and therefore responsible for the administration of Northern Ireland. The police and other services were still under the control of Stormont (NI Parliament) and so when there was a difference of opinion, as there frequently was, then there was nobody to whom we could go and say "Take a decision".

The army in their wisdom had decided that they could police, or they could keep order is a better word, in the very sensitive area in The Falls [Belfast] and in The Bogside in Derry if the police were absent and so they insisted that the police should be withdrawn from both areas.

To be fair, people told me there was never any what you or I would call adequate policing of either The Falls or The Bogside. Before my arrival there were no police in either area, but there had sprung up very efficient and effective vigilante areas—a vigilante patrol in both areas under IRA domination. I thought that the most important thing, and I am sure I was right, was to get the police back into The Falls and Bogside and that is why I used to go in and talk to anybody who would listen to me . . . this is where Craig and Paisley fell out with me right from the beginning. They expected I would take the police in with military support come what may and, if necessary, with the use of arms as had been happening before. I said it couldn't be done this way. I went in to try and placate the feelings of the people and remember it wasn't easy to persuade the people in The Falls

118

when you saw the 400 houses which had been burnt out that the police were coming back.

I had great sympathy with the RUC in those days. In addition their Inspector General who had only been in post for a month had been suspended, and worst of all an Englishman had been imposed upon them. To add to all this, the army were, they thought, their bosses.

After a month or two, it got extremely difficult for me to get out and about because as soon as I was seen anywhere publicly by the Protestants they began a demonstration and sticks and stones were thrown. I am sure if they could they would have liked to have killed me. In Lurgan . . . they made an effigy of Arthur Young and I was burnt publicly. . . Our relationship with the military . . . was a very complex one. During the 13 months I was there I had to deal with no less than seven different generals, all of whom had slightly differing views, all of whom shared the same kind of enthusiasm, but what they could never realise . . . is that Northern Ireland cannot be solved by military force . . . It is a political problem.

One comes to some conclusions I think as a result of experiences in Northern Ireland and elsewhere. One I have already mentioned to you is that military aid to the civil power at the best can prevent the situation from getting worse. It can do nothing to improve it. And military aid independent of police control damages the confidence which the community has in the impartial enforcement of the law and impairs the confidence of the public and the police.

I think the efficiency of any police force anywhere, and we are talking about the democratic state, depends entirely on the amount of confidence which the public has in it.

Endnotes

1. Rawls, op. cit., pp. 453-62
2. Ibid, p. 456
3. Popper, K, *The Open Society and It's Enemies*, Routledge: London. 1991, Vol. 1, Ch. 1
4. Whyte, J, *Interpreting Northern Ireland*, Clarendon: Oxford, 1991, p. 94
5. Popper, K, op. cit., p. 34
6. Whyte, op. cit., p. 18
7. Popper, K, op. cit., p. 9
8. Whyte, op. cit., p. 48
9. Cameron Commission, *Disturbances in Northern Ireland*, Cmd. 532, HMSO: Belfast, 1969, para 6
10. Ibid, para 12
11. Buckland, P, *History of Northern Ireland*, Gill and Macmillan: Dublin, 1981, p. 72
12. Cameron, op. cit., para, 233
13. Whyte, op. cit., p. 195
14. Cameron, op. cit., para. 212
15. Rawls, op. cit., pp. 390-91
16. Bishop and Mallie, *The Provisional IRA*, Corgi: London, 1988, p. 20

17. Ibid, p. 53
18. Hamill, D, *Pig in the Middle,* Methuen: London, 1985, p. 20
19. Whyte, op. cit., p. 256
20. Cameron, op. cit., para. 127
21. Ryder, C, *The RUC: A Force Under Fire*, Methuen: London, 1989, p. 104
22. Cameron, op. cit., para. 44
23. Ibid, para. 53
24. Bishop and Mallie, op. cit., p. 75
25. Clausewitz, *On War*, Penguin: London, 1968, p. 102
26. Clutterbuck, R, *Protest and the Urban Guerrilla*, Cassell: London, 1973, p. 62
27. Cameron Commission, op. cit.
28. Ibid, para. 168
29. Ibid, para. 179
30. Scarman Tribunal of Inquiry, Cmd. 566, HMSO: Belfast, p. 24
31. Ibid, p. 241
32. Ibid, p. 7
33. Ibid, p. 1-8
34. Ibid, p. 16
35. Ibid, p. 15
36. Ibid, p. 15
37. Ibid, p. 15
38. Ibid, p. 16
39. Ibid, p. 17
40. 'European Convention for the Protection of Human Rights and Fundamental Freedoms', article 15
41. Bishop and Mallie, *The Provisional IRA,* Corgi: London, 1988, p. 186
42. Ibid, p. 187
43. Whitelaw, W, *The Whitelaw Memoirs*, Headline: London, 1990, p. 100
44. Hamill, D, op. cit., p. 62
45. Bishop and Mallie, op. cit., p. 165
46. Hamill, D, op. cit., p. 63
47. Ibid, p. 62
48. Taylor, D (Ed.), *The Troubles*, Thames Macdonald: London, 1980, p. 161
49. Widgery, Rt Hon. Lord, Report of Tribunal: H.L. 101 H.C. 220: HMSO p. 38
50. Ibid, p. 38, para. 10
51. Ibid, p. 38, para. 8
52. Ibid, p. 38, para. 5
53. Mill, J S, *On Liberty*, Hacket: Indianapolis, 1978, p. 4
54. European Court of Human Rights, 18 January 1978, Series A, No. 25
55. Cmnd. 535, Belfast: HMSO, 1969.

CHAPTER 6

Disorder and Police in a Well-Ordered Society

In the previous chapter, I discussed problems for 'principled policing' in a society which, in Rawlsian terms, was *not* 'well-ordered.' I will now turn to the restoration of order—and the prospects for principled policing—in a society which, by the same Rawlsian terms, may be described as 'well-ordered'; one in which there is regulation through a public conception of justice which is shared by its members.

Rawls expresses the view that 'systems are more or less stable, depending on the strength of the internal forces that are available to return them to equilibrium'. I agree. It is the power of moral sentiments for justice which strengthen the nature of a social order, just as the lack of such sentiments weaken it. The real test for a 'well-ordered' society then does not lie only in the absence of public protest, organized or spontaneous, or even violent to a degree, but in its capacity for restoring social equilibrium and binding its members once more into a high degree of peaceful social union following protest and disorder.

Change: The only permanence

Societies, being dynamic, are constantly in a state of flux as they seek to arrange and rearrange their affairs. In recent times, in many countries, changes have taken place to improve justice through universal enfranchisement, race relations legislation, measures to prevent discrimination on the grounds of gender, and in relation to employment and concerning age. Thus, a vibrant liberal democracy will seek to be well-ordered by accommodating change. But, since change is often preceded by protest, both peaceful and violent, the need for the enforcement of rules by the state will still be required even though everyone more or less shares the same conceptions of justice. Therefore a well-ordered society will still require policing, and in our terms, principled policing.

Justice: the Best Friend of police

So it is a notion of justice, and the capacity to manifest and maintain just institutions, that determine the stability of society. But even in so-called 'just' societies there remain prospects that from time to time injustices may occur, or be perceived to occur; for societies lack perfection and are dynamic. It is this combination of propensities for injustices and

121

imperfections, together with dynamic social forces, which may from time to time result in social protest, even disorder; a state of affairs which is obviously of primary importance for police. In particular, those societies with institutions and mechanisms for the redress of grievances which are capable of functioning effectively, are less likely to experience prolonged disorder.

Sometimes there are several problems where a sense of grievance is carried forward from historical roots which can be quite powerful, as explained in *Chapter 5*. Such historical forces require fundamental redress or adjustment in order to maintain social stability, as we can see all around us. The socially pluralistic and multi-racial society also generates special needs for those principles and mechanisms which are capable of maintaining order.

In the matter of maintaining a 'well-ordered' society, justice, being the best friend of police, injustice its worst enemy, police should see to it that the part of their role enforcing laws, or using their authority in other ways, is a contribution to justice. If they see that the use of their authority is leading to injustice they should abandon it. In all of this, the behaviour of the police will play a major, if not *the* major role.

LONDON: BRIXTON 1981

To examine the theory of the 'well-ordered' society and its capacity to restore order through justice I propose to take the case of the Brixton riots in London, England in April 1981.

Brixton: A snapshot
Brixton is an established commercial and residential area of South London. It has been in decline since the 1920s and shares some of the features of steady decay, characteristic of many inner-city areas. There are pockets where improvements to property have taken place.

At the time under consideration, over 12,000 dwellings in the London Borough of Lambeth, of which Brixton forms part, were defined as unfit. Twenty-two per cent of housing was owner-occupied, 33 per cent privately rented, and 45 per cent rented from the Council or Housing Association. The population was in decline, being some 246,000, having gone down 20 per cent in five years. There was a strikingly high figure of children in care (2.3 per cent of the population) and single parent families (one in six), twice the national average. The social services expenditure by local authority was the highest in England.

Some 25 per cent of the population belonged to non-white ethnic groups with West Indians being the largest (12.5 per cent). For various reasons, many of these groups had not profited from the educational system, and it was estimated that unemployment among black males under 19 years of age was 55 per cent. It was said by West Indian witnesses to the Scarman Inquiry into the Brixton disorders of April 1981 that:

> Young people around in the streets all day, with nothing to do and nowhere to go, get together in groups, and the "successful" criminal has a story to tell. So one evil has bred another and as unemployment has grown in both older and younger generations, crime has become more commonplace and more acceptable. This is a vicious circle to which there is no end in sight.[2]

The ghetto syndrome

A West Indian sociologist writing at the same time about a community in Bristol similar to that of Brixton, and in which anti-police disorders had occurred, wrote of 'uncompromising postures' of some young male blacks and of their being tied as it were to a 'ghetto way of life', 'characterised by wretchedness, subnormal emotional development, unstable family patterns, and a heavy involvement in such predatory activities as violence, gambling, prostitution, robbery, conning, and living off one's wits'.[3]

The above description might equally well apply to sections of the white community, but there is one very important difference, and that is the question of race and skin colour which is an added complication.

The same writer went on to say that the revolutionary potential of young blacks should not be underestimated:

> They have chosen a criminal path of survival as an expression of their contempt for the system that "puts them down", a stance which exposes them to continuous harassment by the state, represented by the police.

The reader should bear in mind this question of the seemingly uncaring or antagonistic nature of the state which is represented by the police, for the logic is that in order to struggle against society and the state it is necessary to struggle against the police and what they stand for. The police are the visible manifestation of the problem. Police have only to appear to be oppressive or abusive when performing their function for these young people, mainly male, to rationalise a violent reaction.

This situation might be described as the 'ghetto syndrome' wherein people and policing are frequently in conflict by the very nature of things. In order to dissipate some of this mutual antipathy, recourse should be had to principled policing based on the social contract theory, the theory of protectionism (most victims of crime are local residents), and the theory of the common good, as outlined in *Chapter 1*. At some time a fresh start has to be made.

It is remarkable how closely the Scarman Report on the Brixton Disorders describes the conditions in Brixton which were mirrored in the Bristol of the time, as described by Ken Pryce (see *Endnote* 3). Scarman wrote:

> Rightly or wrongly, young black people do not feel politically secure, any more than they feel economically or socially secure . . . And it is regrettably also true that some are tempted by their deprivations into crime, particularly street crime, robbery, car theft, and pick-pocketing offences: in other words, some of them go "mugging". They live their lives on the street having nothing better to do; they make their protest there. The recipe for a clash with the police is ready-mixed; and it takes little or nothing to persuade them that the police, representing an Establishment which they see as insensitive to their plight, are their enemies. [4]

To add to these difficulties at Brixton, the relations between the police and the black community were at a very low ebb at the time of the disorders, for owing to a dispute over policing methods the black leaders had withdrawn from formal dialogue with the police leaders. The Commissioner of Police for the Metropolis was aware that '. . . the relationship with the Lambeth Borough Council [of which Brixton is a part], and the local police had begun to cool!'[5] But nothing effective was done to remedy the situation. Meanwhile the borough area had the highest rate of robbery and violent theft of any area within the Metropolitan Police district, and the fourth highest rate of serious crime. Thus, a part of the community had serious problems with the police, and the police had two problems with that part of the community; firstly its crime rate, and secondly its social, and cultural anxieties leading to alienation.

Street crime and 'Operation Swamp'

In order to counteract the high incidence of street crime and burglary, it was decided by the high police that an operation, called 'Swamp 81', should be launched to strike at the problem.[6] The operation was designed so as to flood Brixton and the surrounding area with mainly young white male police officers in plain clothes working in pairs who were to concentrate on stopping and searching, and persistently and acutely questioning young suspected males, mainly black, between the hours of 2.00 p.m. and 11.00 p.m. for six days. During this operation, 943 individuals were stopped and searched and 118 arrested on suspicion. More than half of those stopped were black, mainly under 21 years of age. The stopping of 825 people without charge would appear to be heavy handed, as only one person was charged with robbery and only one for attempted burglary. During the exercise the police recorded a fall in the reporting of predatory crimes.

The effect of this offensive police action on the young black male community, many of whom felt they were being harassed, was to raise the already tense situation between blacks and police to a more combustible level. Only a spark was needed, and it came on Friday, 10 April 1981, to remind the police to be aware of the sensitivities of people in a community some of whom had reached the limits of tolerance of police behaviour.

On the evening of Friday April 10, two uniformed police officers in a motor vehicle saw a youth in a distressed condition being chased by two or three other black youths. The first youth removed his shirt, and the police saw that he was bleeding from a wound in his back. The police sought to convey him in their car to the hospital, but for some reason he resisted, and other black youths arrived on the scene and began to abuse the police; the injured youth ran away. He was then put in a taxi cab by some members of the public to take him to hospital, but other police officers intervened and began to apply first aid, whereupon they were accused of delaying his journey to hospital and of detaining him. A crowd, mainly black youths, numbering some 30 to 40 gathered and took the young man away from the police (he had not been arrested). He was then taken to hospital by private car.

Crowds now began to stone and throw bottles at the police; police reinforcements arrived, people were being arrested, six police officers were assaulted, and police vehicles were attacked and damaged. Rumours began to spread that the police had deliberately stopped the injured youth from being taken to hospital, and of their being brutal. Local community leaders were now consulted and they advised senior police to diminish their offensive operations.[8] Meanwhile it was decided that 'Operation Swamp' should continue with the stopping of many young blacks frequently and seemingly arbitrarily (Scarman regarded this as an unwise decision).

Riot takes hold

The following day rumours spread amongst the black community that the youth concerned in the incident the night before had died, resulting in heightened tension in the Brixton district.[9]

The next spark leading to disorder involved what can be best described as defective and unprofessional police work. A black taxi driver was detained as a suspect, and even though innocent, was protractedly interrogated, and his taxi searched by two young plain clothes officers in the street in front of a hostile and growing gathering of black youths. Attempts to arrest those abusing them only added to the tension, and officers were assaulted and vehicles stoned; violent disorder on a serious scale began to break out. Throughout the evening and into the night riots took place involving many hundreds of police and violent youths, and there was much damage to property.

Throughout the next day, the police maintained a strong presence amidst scenes of damaged and smouldering property caused during the previous day. The secretary of state for the Home Department, and the police commissioner visited the scene, and were loudly booed by the crowds.

Sporadic violence began to take place and many people were injured. It was reported that 'trouble causers' from other areas had become involved.[10] Initially the commissioner of police blamed the riots on outside influences in the form of a conspiracy, but the subsequent Scarman inquiry found no evidence of this and agreed that it was a spontaneous reaction arising out of the special conditions of Brixton, and the consequences of police misjudgments. The commissioner later withdrew his comments agreeing that the riots were in fact a spontaneous reaction due to the escalation of tensions brought about by the police tactics. He reported the following details:

> Between Friday 10 April, and Monday 13 April 1981, 415 police officers and 172 members of the public were injured. 118 police vehicles and 61 private vehicles were damaged. 4 police vehicles and 30 private vehicles were destroyed. 28 premises were seriously damaged by fire and a further 158 premises were attacked.[11]

Studying these events in Brixton in April 1981 cannot but lead one to regard the riotous behaviour as the outcome of difficult social conditions, producing hostile attitudes, later inflamed by the actions of police, who, in recent times, had become mistrusted and even hated by some sections of the black community.

I had earlier (1979)[12] warned that 'The decaying inner-city areas are breeding grounds of crime and disaffection. To leave the problem to the vagaries of law enforcement would be unwise . . .' I reinforced those views during visits to my police command from the home secretary, government ministers, and the Commissioner of Police for the Metropolis, but was unable to make the kind of headway which, ironically, only became possible after the riots had taken place. Few of my senior colleagues were supportive of my community policing views at this time.

It would not amount to a satisfactory and adequate explanation of the violent disorders in Brixton in 1981 merely to describe economic and social difficulties faced by some black youths, for many white people faced similar problems. But it is the extra dimension of race which makes a difference, as Scarman wrote:

> The black community in Brixton faces similar problems to those facing the white community, but more severe. The family, education, unemployment and discrimination are particular areas of difficulty. As a result young black people may feel a particular sense of frustration and deprivation. Spending much of their lives on the street, they are bound to come into contact with criminals and with the police.[13]

These were not race riots, nor can the violence be condoned. Protest, as Martin Luther King manifested, is more effective where it is peaceful and persistent. The Brixton riots were an outburst of anger and resentment, though the police bore no responsibility for the social malaise, but Scarman was quite sure that

> . . . unless the police adjust their policies and operation so as to handle these difficulties with imagination as well as firmness, they will fail, and disorder will become a disease endemic in our society.[14]

This last comment is of primary importance in the art of policing in a plural multi-racial society. It represents a challenge to the whole idea of principled policing. It is not enough for policing to take up a legalistic posture under the Rule of Law, even though such a position appears virtuous enough. The keeping of the peace in a complicated social order requires of police that it be achieved through policing which is skilfully fashioned, directed, and applied.

Return to equilibrium
At the beginning of this chapter I mentioned that the capacity of a society to restore a just peace and social function following public disorder will indicate whether or not it is a 'well-ordered' society within the Rawlsian meaning of the term. As Rawls comments:

> Since in practice all social systems are subjected to disturbances of some kind, they are practically stable, let us say, if the departures from their preferred equilibrium positions caused by normal disturbances elicit forces sufficiently strong to restore these equilibra . . .[15]

The forces being referred to in the present context include a political will to reform—and a general public sympathy for principles of justice to be invoked in the redress of any genuine grievance. Such forces would be no impediment to the prosecution of criminal offences, for without the will to enforce the law where necessary, a just conclusion would not be possible, for justice would not be done or seen to be done.

Political will

After the riots had subsided it would have been politically inept to leave the matter in the hands of the police. What was required as the first step towards recovery of equilibrium was a political initiative, a gesture of intent.

In the Brixton case the first reaction of the government was the setting up of an independent inquiry, the Scarman Inquiry, to which I have already referred. On 13 April 1981, the day following the riots, the home secretary announced in a statement to the House of Commons his intention of appointing Lord Scarman, Lord of Appeal, a senior, much respected, and humane judge, to carry out an inquiry '. . . urgently into the serious disorder on 10-12 April 1981, with the power to make recommendations', Lord Scarman later informed me that he could only accept the home secretary's invitation if it were agreed that he should make recommendations, rather than merely present a report. In this, as with many things, Lord Scarman manifested his wisdom.

What Lord Scarman said

In his report,[16] Lord Scarman described the social conditions in Brixton before going on to examine the policing at Brixton at the time. He found that the disorders were criminally riotous, but were not premeditated, and not race riots. 'The riots were essentially an outburst of anger and resentment of young black people against the police'.

After referring to the dilemma of the rising volume of crime, and the problem for the police in combatting this, he placed responsibility for the breakdown of local relationships fairly and squarely on the local community leaders and local police. He had much to say about the need for considerable improvements in police recruitment, discipline, and policing methods—but the central thrust of his report was the subject of police consultation with communities, and police accountability. He recommended that a legal duty should be placed upon police authorities and chief officers of police to set-up consultative arrangements with the various communities within their jurisdictions.

I agreed fully with Lord Scarman's recommendation for the setting up of the foundations for what we had by then begun to call 'community policing', which flows from our social contract theory of police and our 'principled policing'. In my own written evidence to Lord Scarman's inquiry I made the following comments:

A new social contract for police

Community policing requires three elements, Community Police Councils (Consultative Groups), inter-agency cooperation, and community constables appointed to localities, and this arrangement in turn requires committed leadership and wide dissemination of information to the public at large — a truly participatory scheme of things.

It is because our principled policing theory seeks in practice to do justice, that it evolves as superior to mere law enforcement or the maintenance of order for their own sakes. Lord Scarman, the home secretary, and the prime minister agreed with this, as will be seen.

What the commissioner of police said[17]

In his memoirs the Commissioner of the Metropolitan Police wrote: 'If the location [Brixton] was predictable so was the immediate cause of the violence—antagonism towards the police'. And events '. . . only underlined the sad state of relationships between Brixton's black community and Brixton's police officers'. 'From a police point of view it was much like a war'.

When the home secretary informed the commissioner of his intention to set up the Scarman inquiry into the policing of Brixton, the commissioner recorded his serious reservations and described his meeting with the secretary of state and senior civil servants as being 'acrimonious'. The politics of the situation, he recorded, 'haunts me still', as '. . . the police were put into the dock'. He declined to give evidence personally to the Scarman inquiry, being represented by a senior colleague.

There is little doubt that the policeman and the politician revealed the differences in instincts and judgment. A political solution was urgently called for and this was a case where I agreed with the politician.

What the home secretary said[18]

In his account of events the home secretary wrote:

I toured the area . . . with the Metropolitan Police Commssioner. There were scenes of appalling damage and I felt I was back in the war during the London blitz or fighting in a town on North-West Europe.

'We needed an independent inquiry'; 'I also knew I could not expect the Commissioner of the Metropolitan Police to be enthusiastic about a judicial inquiry. He was bound to feel this was a matter for the police themselves'.

What the prime minister said[19]
In her memoirs, the prime minister wrote:

> I accepted Willy Whitelaw's suggestion that Lord Scarman, the
> distinguished Law Lord, should undertake an inquiry into the causes of
> what happened and make recommendations.

Dismissing criticisms of her economic policies, she said of other
allegations that '. . . racial minorities were reacting to police brutality and
racial discrimination we took more seriously'.

Following the Scarman report, 'We introduced a statutory
framework for consultation between the police and local authorities,
tightened the rules on stopping and searching suspects, and brought in
other measures relating to police recruitment, training and discipline'.

Scarman report presented to Parliament
When presenting the Scarman report to the House of Commons on 17
November 1981, the home secretary, William Whitelaw, accepted its
general principles, and particularly endorsed the detailed arrangements
proposed for ensuring what might be described as social contractual
dimension for policing:

> Lord Scarman's detailed recommendations on policing policy arrangements
> add up to a statement of philosophy and direction for the future which rests
> on the need for the police to carry out their duty with the consent and the
> support of the community.

During the debate on the report, after stressing the obvious need for the
police vigorously to tackle street crime, the home secretary committed
the government to immediate establishment of local community liaison
or consultative committees. Henceforth the principles of policing would
include a formal and permanent dialogue with communities to enable
their 'special needs' to be addressed. The idea of carrying out the
policing function of 'keeping of the peace' in a plural society with a
respectful recognition of that pluralism provided important progress in
the nature of policing for the common good. It was now time to turn
political rhetoric into law followed by police action.

Implementation
The politicians having shown the political will to provide for a return to
equilibrium, attention now focused on the police, and particularly on
their leaders for implementation of the political intentions. The
willingness and skill of the police to implement all this could not be
taken for granted. In the first place there was a feeling among police that

they had not been to blame for the Brixton riots, and that the advocates of change favoured what critics called 'soft policing' as if that lacked what some would later describe as 'zero-tolerance'; in other words unremitting and hardline police tactics, the very tactics which sparked off the Brixton riots in the first place.

The foregoing attitude of course manifests a distorted view through the prism of policing. There are circumstances when an unrelenting strategy of law enforcement is called for, but this should not be done without public support which, in turn, requires good communication from police to public. To facilitate progress in this field, the Scarman report set out clear objectives, as later did the Police and Criminal Evidence Act 1984, section 67, and relevant Home Office guidance.

The need to anticipate and to frustrate crime is also an essential element in advanced police strategy and tactics, though it is often less spectacular than equating the police function with 'war' and 'victories'.

To achieve progress in this field it is necessary to enhance progressive police education, training, and leadership. As Lord Scarman said about modern policing in Britain:

> If their policing is such that it can be seen to be the application to our new (multi-racial and plural) society of the traditional principles of British policing, the risk of unrest will diminish, and the prospect of approval by all responsible elements in our ethnically diverse society will be greater. If they neglect consultation and cooperation with the local community, unrest is certain, and riot becomes probable.[20]

With these wise comments in mind I will turn to consider a form of basic everyday policing strategy which fulfils theories of 'principled policing' and meets the demands of the Scarman report also.

Community policing

As I have already noted, the population of Brixton was heterogeneous, and had a significant proportion of transient residents. This kind of community is a difficult one to police where the system of policing seeks to establish a rapport with public diversity. As trustees of the people's police under the social contract theory the police have to be more imaginative—as Scarman enjoined them to be. But this imagination must include firm policing methods and effective enforcement of laws.

Principled policing under the social contract includes that of protectionism which encompasses defence of residents against criminal activity, but it is to the theory of policing the common good that policies should be directed. Brixton therefore seems to suggest that it was the kind of community for which a system of community policing might be more successful than that based solely on a reactive law enforcement model. It was because of this, that I presented evidence to the Scarman Inquiry which suggested such a course.[21]

Community policing requires the following elements:

- community police consultative committees
- inter-agency cooperation; and
- community police constables appointed to localities.

The objectives of the system include cooperative action for the prevention of crime, united support in reducing fear of crime, and the creation of reinforcement of trust in neighbourhoods. Since the system is based mainly on better organization of existing resources, it does not require excessive funding. The force of law may be required to establish necessary change.

Since community policing is preventive social organization and a consultative enterprise, it calls for inter-ministerial sponsorship. Home affairs, health, social security, education and environment are ministries which should jointly address the system. An advisory department for policing community affairs should be formed. Social work, education, youth, community welfare, probation services, health, planning and housing are services whose cooperation is essential for effective community policing. Non-government organizations and voluntary bodies also have an important part to play.

The community police organization provides the roots for the sound growth of effective policing. The trunk and branches represent more familiar police functions of emergency patrols, public order maintenance, and criminal investigation.

It is through a well established system of community policing that the optimum conditions towards positive and constructive activity are likely to be created. The public, perceiving that the police care for and respect their own group or culture are encouraged to—and if given information and trust will—help the police to achieve their goals. It is important that the simple formula of community policing becomes part of the police culture and of their general understanding.

CONCLUSION

At the beginning of this chapter I suggested that a 'well-ordered' society was one with a capacity for restoring social equilibrium and binding its members once more into a high degree of peaceful social union following protest and disorder. From the above inquiry it would seem that British society emerged from the aftermath of the Brixton riots as a 'well-ordered' one.

The Scarman Inquiry: A postscript

To add support to the findings of the Scarman Inquiry, if support be needed, it is of interest to note the report of the Advisory Commssion on Civil Disorders established by the President of the United States, Lyndon B Johnson,[22] following severe riotous disturbances in many US cities during the years 1963-1967, when many people were killed and billions of dollars worth of damage was done. In 1967, 150 cities reported disruptions, eight of which were major riots and another 33 of which were serious disturbances.

The report known as the Kerner Report—after the name of the head of the inquiry—recorded on a much larger scale many of the characteristics of what I earlier described as 'ghetto syndrome'. First of all there is the culmination of such things as unemployment, social disorganization, poverty, crime, exploitation of consumers, particular health problems, and the impossibility of breaking out of this.

Most crime, it was said, was committed by only a small minority of residents and the principal victims of crime were also residents of similar neighbourhoods. There was extreme tension between communities and the police, described as 'deep hostility between police and ghetto communities which was a primary cause of the disorders'. In addition to physical and verbal abuse the report listed some of the other police practices such as discourtesy, indiscriminate stop and search (Operation Swamp, Brixton), breaking up street groups, aggressive preventive patrols, motorisation of the police, and other dissonances.[23]

As in the Scarman report, the Kerner Commission concluded that 'the police bear a major responsibility for making needed changes', and also dismissed suggestions that the riots were the result of a conspiracy. The conspiracy theory, if borne out by fact, would have shifted some of the blame.

Endnotes

1. Scarman, Lord, *The Brixton Disorders*, 10-12 April 1981, Cmnd. 8427, HMSO: London, 1981. Part II of this Report contains a profile of the Brixton area at the time.
2. Ibid, para. 2. 23
3. Pryce, K, *Endless Pressure*, Penguin: London, 1979, p. 276
4. Scarman, op. cit., paras. 2.36-2.37
5. Evidence of the Commissioner of Police of the Metropolis to Scarman, p. 57
6. Scarman, op. cit., para. 4. 37
7. Ibid, para. 3. 4
8. Ibid, para. 3. 2
9. Ibid, para. 3. 29
10. Ibid, para. 3. 101
11. McNee, Sir D, *McNee's Law*, Collins: London, 1983, p. 111
12. Alderson, J, *Policing Freedom*, Macdonald and Evans: Plymouth, 1979, p. 177

13. Scarman, op. cit., para. 8. 5
14. Ibid, para. 9. 2
15. Rawls, J, *Justice as Fairness*, Oxford University Press: Oxford, 1973
16. Cmnd. 8427, HMSO: London, 1981
17. McNee, op. cit., p. 109
18. Whitelaw, W, *The Whitelaw Memoirs*, Headline: London, 1990, p. 243
19. Thatcher, M, *The Downing Street Years*, Harper Collins: London, 1995, p. 143
20. Scarman, op. cit., para. 8. 5
21. Alderson, J, *Law and Disorder*, Hamish Hamilton: London, 1984, Appendix
22. Kerner Report—'President's Advisory Committee on Civil Disorders', Bantam: New York, 1968.

CHAPTER 7

Political Morality and the Policing of Revolt

In this chapter I want to examine the vexed question of the role of the state in relation to distributive justice, and the implication of its policies for principled policing. When the policies of government, even in a well-ordered state, are perceived to be unjust, they may cause anger leading to revolt, and this has obvious and important implications for principled policing. To examine this phenomenon I have chosen the British miners strike of 1984-1985.

THE BRITISH MINERS STRIKE: 1984 - 1985

The course of the miners strike was exceedingly complex with a close interweaving of several plots and sub-plots, personalities, events and external circumstances; central to the array of developments, however, was the role of the police, and the manner in which they carried out their duties. This is a 'play within a play'. The play is the story of the economic and industrial policies of the Conservative government (1979-84), and the play within it is that of the industrial conflict between the National Union of Mineworkers and the National Coal Board, in which a major political role is played by the police. I will deal with each in turn.

There are other important roles represented by the non-striking miners, and various shadowy influences manipulating some of the forces at play for their several purposes.[1] There is considerable literature on the subject, some of it listed in the *Bibliography*. Here I am primarily concerned with that part of the drama involving the police.

I will examine the politics in due course, meanwhile it should be noted that, to paraphrase Clausewitz, policing is an extension of politics by other means. This being so, the morality of politics bears on the morality of police.

Should the politics be seen to be constitutional and moral, then the matter is uncomplicated. Should they be seen to be unconstitutional and unjust the matter is also uncomplicated, since the politics are not only blatantly immoral, but they are seen to be so. In both the cases the police know where they stand. But, where the politics are constitutional and in the main legally proper, but regarded as unjust, unfair or immoral, then at least—so far as the police are concerned—the matter becomes very complicated.

Where the coercive arm of government is deployed in a major way to help the government achieve an unjust objective, or a just objective by unjust means, then, by association, the police become despised, and are thereby diminished. Should the police be protractedly engaged in this way they become exposed to cynicism, and to ethical corruption; and this may lead to a lowering of standards of discipline, and of personal and group behaviour.

High police officials, when considering the wide ranging nature of policing tasks, will understand the political nature of the events upon which they are to embark. After all, it is the government which is responsible for the general state of law and order in the land, and the police are to carry out their tasks within the boundaries of the laws, which are also political instruments.

The foregoing are just some of the characteristics of the subject confronting us, but first of all it is necessary to have regard to the uniqueness of the mining fraternity, and its community, for this may explain much to anyone unfamiliar with the subject. For those of us who have lived in and policed miners, and mining communities, there is no doubt that in many respects they differ from other industrial and commercial workers and their neighbourhoods. Without an understanding of the miners, it will not be easy to understand the turn of events which overwhelmed their industry and their way of life in Britain in 1984.

Miners

A scheme of social cooperation should generate stability, and a sense of justice is essential to that end, otherwise, as Rawls puts it:

> Distrust and resentment corrode the ties of civility, and suspicion and hostility tempt men to act in ways they would otherwise avoid.[2]

It is a characteristic of miners that they have a tremendous sense of loyalty to each other. Working together in dangerous and unpleasant conditions, they depend upon each other for their safety, and often their survival. This sense of obligation is *par excellence* a moral contractual one, and one which is carried out from the mines into the communities, tightly knit against misfortunes as they are. Their women and children carry on where the menfolk leave off, as witness their rallying around in times of adversity, such as a prolonged strike, with food kitchens, welfare help for the aged, the children, and even those voluntary bodies called 'Police-watch' who were out to monitor the behaviour of the police.

Miners were early participants in the growth of Friendly Societies which represented a mutuality of help for each other and each other's dependents, in sickness and in death, due to occupational accidents. It is of special interest as showing the efforts made by the workmen, long before it was decided by Parliament, in 1897, that the liability was one which the employer should be called upon to bear.

Paul Routledge, political correspondent and biographer of Arthur Scargill, himself a Yorkshireman and the product of a mining family and community wrote:

> ... their industry for which they had sacrificed so much through generation after generation, had fuelled the Industrial Revolution and the nation's prosperity. Their hard way of life is tough, proud communities were legendary ... It was not just an industry it was a way of life.[3]

In his much respected account, *INJUSTICE: The Social Bases of Obedience and Revolt*, Barrington Moore (1978) provides us with interesting comments on aspects of the experience of German miners, which offers contrasts and comparisons with the British experience. The German miners' tradition, as in all those known to the author, was to work in what were called *Kameradschaften*, or, in English, 'comradely groups'.

Until the middle of the nineteenth century the German miners were a guild which 'remained embedded in corporate paternalism', in which they had 'pride a sense of honour' with a recognised status in the German social order. They had exemption from certain taxes, and their working conditions were under state protection. In case of illness of themselves or of accidents, they and their families were provided with grants and benefits. Nothing comparable in any way existed in Britain at the time, where it was quite common practice for women, and children as young as seven years of age to be employed in the mines.

Between 1851 and 1865 however, the German miners began to lose most of their former privileges *'as the mine owners became free to exploit the industry'* and *'. . . the miners found themselves at the not so tender mercies of the laws of supply and demand in a free market'*[4] (Emphasis supplied); most British miners were always at these 'not so tender mercies'.

> In order to meet the demands of the market the mine owners tried to impose more rigid and bureaucratic controls . . . which created resentment [as the miners] carried their past with them into the new [industrial] age.[5]

The British miners also carried their past with them into the new Thatcherite age.

The great German miners strike of 1889 turned into 'a major political event'. Not all the miners went on strike, and as a general rule, those who refused to strike worked in the more paternalistically managed mines, which on the face of it is more comparable to the Nottinghamshire miners in the strikes of 1926 and 1984.

Moore believed the German miners 'were trying to change the terms of the prevailing contract', which caused the disputing parties 'to act in a shadowy area where there is no generally accepted boundary between morally approved and reprehensible behaviour'.[6] This question of the morality of behaviour was also a big issue in the British strike of 1984.

The next German miners strike took place in 1905, though wages were not the prime issue. The causes of the strike included the arbitrary nature of discipline, immigrant workers, and the Coal Syndicate's decision to close down some mines which threatened some 10,000 jobs of those established miners who had their own cottages and plots of land. This issue of threats to jobs and to the living environment was that which propelled the British miners to strike in 1984.

It is also interesting to note Moore's comments about German union members who were likened to

> . . . the great mercenary generals of the Thirty Years War who often sought big armies as the basis for power and prestige, but tried to avoid big battles because they were expensive and dangerous.[7]

This analogy with the military and war was to characterise statements made by the opposing leaders during the British strike of 1984, e.g. in the rhetoric of the chairman of the National Coal Board when referring to the union leader and his 'storm troopers'.

When the German employers pronounced that the demands of the miners and their leaders represented an intolerable infringement on the 'prerogative of management', they used the very words which were frequently to be echoed by the senior management of the British National Coal Board in 1984.

Throughout the German strike, Moore tells us, the German miners failed to extract any concessions from the employers; a situation which once more was reflected in the later British experience.

There was little to report by way of violence and the threat of mass picketing in the German case, as opposed to the British in 1984. There was considerable public sympathy for the German miners, and after their strike, trade union membership increased considerably; the reverse was the case with the British National Union of Mineworkers, the Union which led the 1984 strike. The miners of the highly profitable Nottinghamshire coalfield were unreliable when it came to industrial action. In the General Strike of 1926 they broke away from the NUM to form their own non-striking union; the same was to happen in 1984-1985, and Ian MacGregor, encouraged by the government, was ruthlessly to exploit this division. The other fissure in the NUM strategy (if they had one) was their failure to hold a national ballot, but this in no way excused the government from contriving their humiliation.

Forebodings

On 9 January 1972, during the period of the Conservative government of Ted Heath, the NUM called for an all-out strike concerning pay. For the first and only time in the history of coalmining the strike was solid; 280,000 miners at 289 pits struck as one. This strike took place against an economic background made difficult by the onset of an oil crisis which resulted from the Six-day War in the Middle East. It was at this time that the president of the Yorkshire area of the miners union, Arthur Scargill, emerged as a militant political activist of some influence.

Events at Saltley Coke Depot in Birmingham provided a scenario which established the effectiveness of mass secondary picketing over traditional policing methods. The Yorkshire miners' leader, Arthur Scargill, was able to assemble some 3,000 striking miners and other trade unionists from amongst engineering workers in Birmingham. Arthur Scargill recalls that the then chief constable, Sir Derek Capper, decided to close the gates of the coke depot and stop the convoys of lorries from transporting the coke to its industrial users. At the request of the chief constable who was apprehensive of violence, Arthur Scargill, taking a police megaphone, gave a political speech to the assembled workers telling them it was the greatest victory of the working class in his lifetime.

Paul Routledge reports Scargill as saying:

> Here was the living proof that the working class only had to flex its muscles and it could bring governments, employers, society, to a total standstill. I know the fear of Birmingham on the part of the ruling class. The fear was that what happened in Birmingham could happen in every city in Britain.[8]

These words were to have a striking effect on the attitudes of future Conservative governments. The government's response to the strike at this time was unusually swift. It set up an Inquiry under Lord Wilberforce.

The inquiry quickly concluded that the miners had lost ground in wages, and that it was in the national interest to have a viable coal industry, and an efficient work force. It awarded substantial pay rises for the miners which the government soon paid. But the continuing impact of the Middle-East oil crisis on the government's policy of wage restraint failed to go away.

Early in 1974, with discontent over wages still rumbling on, the miners leaders called another strike. By this time the prime minister, Ted

Heath, took the risky course of calling a General Election in defiance of trades union pressure on pay, with the slogan 'Who Governs Britain?' He lost the election to the Labour party under Harold Wilson.

William Whitelaw, who was secretary of state for employment, under Ted Heath, later said that '. . . inside and outside the Conservative party the defeat [by the miners] was seen as a humiliation for the government', and 'there was a feeling in many quarters that the organized power of the miners was too strong to resist'.[9]

Miners and Thatcherism

When Margaret Thatcher's Conservative government was elected in 1979, strategic planning began immediately to ensure mastery over the miners in any future conflict. But much to her consternation her government was soon to be in dispute with the NUM over the subject of pit closures on economic grounds. Not feeling themselves to be in a strong enough position to defy the NUM demands, they gave way. Although this was a further galling experience and climb down for a Conservative government, it only served to stiffen their resolve to slay the dragon of the NUM, given a future opportunity, which was to come in 1984. Mrs Thatcher was clearly angry with the NCB in 1981. She wrote:

> Far from acting as management might be expected to do the National Coal Board was behaving as if it entirely shared the interests of the union representing its employees.[10]

She considered these relationships to be an extraordinary legacy of state socialism. There was no empathy or sympathy in her manner as the ultimate employer of the miners whom she later dubbed 'the enemy within', seeking to place the miners, and in particular their leaders, alongside other enemies of her country such as General Galtieri, the Argentine dictator, whom she vanquished in the Falkland Islands.

Realising that the NCB had entered into a battle with the miners which they could not win, she had even less confidence in their management. It became clear to her that all she could do was cut her losses and live to fight another day. This would give time to prepare to resist and to win the next, and inevitable conflict with the coal miners, as the government determined to make the coal industry profitable.

As part of its strategy for dealing with the nationalised industries, should it come to power, the Conservative party had in 1979 produced a report, later known as the Ridley Report (after its author Nicholas Ridley MP) which amongst other things was to prepare the way for a major confrontation with the miners. The government would build up coal stocks at the point of delivery, arrange the importation of coal, encourage

140

non-union transport, and introduce oil-firing as alternative fuel in all power stations; large forces of suitably equipped police should be arranged to control picketing. Margaret Thatcher records details of all these preparations in her memoirs.

The police
It is an irony of the history of the miners dispute that had anti-police riots not occurred in London's Brixton and the racially sensitive areas in urban England in 1981, there would have been no highly trained or equipped public order police ready to mount an aggressive operation against miners' assemblies and mass pickets in the 1984 miners strike.

As recently as 1980, a Home Office paper on *Public Order* explained:

> The British police do not have sophisticated riot equipment—such as tear gas or water cannon to handle demonstrators. Their traditional approach is to deploy large numbers of officers in ordinary uniform in the passive containment of a crowd. Neither the government or the police wish to see this approach abandoned in favour of more aggressive methods.[11]

Exceptionally high levels of ability, confidence and inspiration, are called for in political leaders and high police command if they are to turn unpropitious social circumstances, involving marginalised people—including those marginalised *pro-tem* as in a strike—into circumstances in which violent conflict between police and people is rendered less probable.

Police violence cannot be morally justified unless conditions render reconciliatory tactics impossible. A principle of the obligation to keep the people's peace is to mollify conflict between factions.

It does not require great imagination to design a tough and aggressive arm of the state with which to subdue and intimidate economic, social or cultural 'underclasses', and those who become despised through propaganda. One problem with such policies is the sowing of the 'dragon's teeth' of future civic discord and violence. Any government whose policies create turbulence and potent rebellious entities will always have to invest heavily in the power of coercion. As a French police colleague said to me, 'France is the country of the revolution so we must have a powerful police system to maintain *l'ordre publique*'.

The English police idea on the other hand, where the police are 'the people's' posits a different philosophical concept, which serves to inhibit the scope of governments to indulge in unnecessary confrontations of power politics. 'Misuse of the ruler's instruments of violence against their own subjects is an extreme violation of the obligation to keep the peace'.[13]

It is an observable fact that the characteristics of a state at any point in time are manifested in the characteristics of its police. Thus a nation at ease with itself, and in which people and government enjoy some degree of harmony, will require less in the way of public-order police resources than a state where government manifests confrontational characteristics. As one political commentator put it, in relation to the Thatcher administration (1979-84):

> In social welfare and industrial policy a curious force of indirect rule in which neutral non-government institutions such as the police [sic], the courts, or the nationalised industries are pushed into the front line to fight political battles, something which has put serious strains on social organizations, and politicised much which is traditionally apolitical.[14]

It would never occur to a Frenchman to refer to the French police as a non-government institution, and to do so in the British context only goes to typify the British idea that the police are not an arm of *the* government, though they are an arm of government. This is more than a subtle play on words.

Due to the social turbulence created amongst the black minorities of England's inner-city areas, the police idea was to be propelled into preparedness against future such disorders. Changes followed recommendations of the Scarman Inquiry into the Brixton Disorders of 10-12 April 1981 (*Chapter 6*). These recommendations included the need for:

1. Sufficient properly trained and equipped officers available for rapid reinforcement
2. More effective protective equipment for officers—including better helmets, flameproof clothing, and perhaps lighter shields.

Out of these sensible suggestions emerged a fresh arm of policing which was quite alien to the British tradition, but was one which had been developed to control and contain public order in the colonies of the British Empire, and before that in Ireland under British rule. Although Sir Robert Peel when Chief Secretary for Ireland (1812-18) introduced colonial style police called Peace Preservation Forces, he refused to introduce this style of policing in London in 1829, believing that only a far less aggressive policing model would be acceptable in England. Of course military aid to the civil power was not infrequently used in those days, much to the dislike of the Duke of Wellington.

The chief constables based their design of the new public order police function on the colonial police manuals, and on advice from the Royal Hong Kong Police. Strangely for a democratic society, the new

142

Police Public Order Manual was classified as 'secret' and was not even made available to members of Parliament, which seems and odd way to go about things.

The new police arm was first to be tested, not by a resurgence of inner-city disorder, but by the outcome of the confrontational industrial policies of the government and the National Coal Board, together with the protests of the National Union of Mineworkers. The public image of the British police was to undergo a transformation. During the miners strike, millions of television viewers daily watched scenes of violence between the police and picketing miners. The 'people's police' seemed more and more to be the 'government's police'.

Mrs Thatcher's government now had at its disposal a police arm which could be deployed in the mining communities where the menfolk were on strike, and where the women were out in support. No longer would a conservative government bewail the need for a tough police. The police model was now available to strengthen the power of central government, whilst at the same time tending to weaken police loyalties and affinities with local government, mining communities, and the so-called working classes of the people.

Rawls reminds us that '. . . although a society is a cooperative venture for mutual advantage, it is typically marked by conflict as well as by an identity of interests'.[15]

Policing is concerned with the balance between cooperation and conflict in order that the people's peace should prevail. Where the degree of conflict markedly exceeds that of cooperation, then the police, noting the imbalance, should seek ways of restoring the balance as peacefully as possible. Should the police and others concerned be unable to do this, then violence followed by reactionary violence is adumbrated. The British miners strike was to manifest this dilemma dramatically.

The politics
It is essential at this stage to note that at the time of the British miners strike of 1984-85, the coal industry was in public ownership, having been nationalised by the Labour government in 1947. For almost 40 years the miners had grown accustomed to dealing with governments as employers in such matters as the state of the industry, their working conditions, wages, allowances, and terms of employment. These circumstances were inclined to induce a sense of partnership in the minds of the employees, but critically, any dispute between the miners and the employers, namely the government of the day, automatically became, not simply as industrial dispute, but a political issue. The miners strike of 1984-85 was therefore a political issue, and the policing of it was *ipso facto* a political task, and this on the face of it cast the police

143

as the government's coercive arm.

Principled police should bear in mind the social contractual relationship which they have with the miners as well as with the government; further, that policing has to have regard for the common good, including the good of the striking miners, as well as the good of the working miners, and not just the good of the rest of society.

As the coal industry developed under public ownership, so did other public utilities including railways, steel, hospitals, and medical services of the National Health Service, which had also been part of the post-war Labour government's nationalisation and socialist programme. During this period of public ownership the relevant trade unions had become very powerful and able to challenge the authority of governments—who, as stated, were ultimately their employers.

The Conservative government of 1979 embarked on a programme of reform to transfer publicly owned industries and utilities back to the private sector, and in addition to reform the trade union movement.

Labour governments had hesitated to reform the trade unions, though steps had been taken in this direction during the Labour government of Harold Wilson in 1969, specifically in the White Paper, *In Place of Strife* advanced by Barbara Castle, minister of employment. The issue was divisive amongst the Labour party ranks and reforms were cautious. It was felt by many people that the Labour Party had left too much in the matter of trades union reform to the Conservatives, and Mrs Thatcher rose to the occasion with enthusiastic zeal. Her reforms were both fundamental and astringent, and were greatly helped by public disenchantment, following a plethora of strikes by public services, which so inconvenienced and disrupted the life of the country in 1979 that it became known as 'The Winter of Discontent'.

Succeeding the Labour government in 1979, the Conservatives took the first steps along the political path sometimes referred to as 'Mrs Thatcher's Revolution'.[16] For present purposes, we are concerned only with those policies of the government which impinged on the coal mining industry, heralding the conflict between the National Coal Board (the government) and the National Union of Mineworkers, which created the protracted bad tempered year long dispute which involved the police, both contentiously and non-contentiously.

In their manifesto for the General Election of 1983, the Conservative party had declared:

> Both trade union members and the general public have welcomed the 1980 and 1982 Employment Acts, which restrain secondary picketing [a big issue in the 1984 strike] encourage secret ballots [also contentious during the strike] curtail abuse of the closed shop, and restore rights of redress against trades unions responsible for committing unlawful acts.

144

They further promised to give union members the right to hold ballots for the election of governing bodies of the unions, and to decide periodically whether their unions should have party political funds. They also indicated that the legal immunity of unions to cause strikes without prior approval by means of a member's secret ballot would be curbed (this resolution was the subject of the Trades Union Act 1984). This measure came into force during the strike, too late to affect the failure to ballot in 1984.

Significantly for the nationalised industries, the government declared its intention to '. . . expose state-owned firms to real competition'. Depending on how this was to be carried out it had much potential for causing uncertainties amongst the miners.

The National Coal Board
On 1 September 1983, Ian MacGregor was appointed chairman of the National Coal Board. He turned out to be the kind of person Mrs Thatcher had been looking for to manage reform of the coal industry to a market competitive condition.

The NUM had already been informed that between 65,000 and 70,000 jobs had to go over the next five years through the closure of 'uneconomic pits', and an overtime ban by the NUM was in force at the time in protest.

MacGregor had worked in US industry for more than 40 years where he gained a reputation as a strike breaker.[17] He brought with him to his new task what is called the Mohawk Valley Formula, a 'scientific' approach to strike-breaking. The six key elements of this formula have some bearing on the ethical nature of management, and are therefore set out here in full.[18]

1. When a strike is threatened label the Union leaders as 'agitators' to discredit them with the public and their own followers . . .
2. Disseminate propaganda, by means of press releases, advertisements, and the activities of the missionaries; such propaganda must stress the arbitrary demands of strikers . . .
3. Align the influential members of the community into a cohesive group opposed to the strike. Include in this group, usually designated a Citizens Committee, representatives of the bankers, real estate owners, and businessmen . . .
4. Bring about the formation of a large armed police force to intimidate the strikers and to exert a psychological effect upon the citizens . . . [MacGregor undertook this personally as we shall see].
5. Most important heighten the demoralising effect of the above measures — all designed to convince the strikers that their cause is hopeless — by a 'back-to-work' movement, operated by a puppet association of so called 'loyal employees' secretly organized by the employer. The association

wages a publicity campaign in its own name and coordinates such campaign with the work of the missionaries circulated among the strikers and visiting their homes.

6. Close the publicity barrage which day by day during the entire period has increased demoralisation worked by all of these measures on the theme that the plant is in full operation and that the strikers are merely a minority attempting to interfere with the right to work, thus inducing the public to place a moral stamp of approval upon the above measures. With this, the campaign is over—the employer has broken the strike.

According to his own version of events[19] MacGregor held a discussion with the prime minister about his strategy of attrition to beat the NUM and Scargill its leader into submission when the anticipated strike broke out; this, together with the government's careful stockpiling and strategic arrangements for the availability of a diversity of fuels, was in essence the plan which then allied to the policing strategy mentioned at item 4 in the above list would bring about the government's triumph.

Mrs Thatcher always knew that it was pit closures that were more likely to ignite a strike than a dispute about pay. Mr MacGregor had already told the prime minister that he would dictate the outbreak of industrial confrontation, saying, 'I must warn you that it could be a long and rough ride. And I would suggest that if you don't see it that way you should tell me now, before we start down the path'.[20] The prime minister apparently 'saw it that way'.

The events which followed were tortuous, complicated, controversial, and full of passion to the end. There is now a very large body of literature on the subject some of which is mentioned in the *Bibliography*. I am however indebted to the work of Jonathan and Ruth Winterton for much detailed information contained in their meticulous account.[21]

Meanwhile MacGregor began to apply his 'Mohawk Valley' tactics by vilifying his opponents, and even Mrs Thatcher began to refer to the striking miners as the 'enemy within' (incidentally, the title of MacGregor's memoirs). Those who opposed him were people 'with malice in their hearts',[22] and Scargill was a 'publicity seeking Marxist'. 'We put together a sort of war cabinet',[23] he wrote, but he complained of resistance form senior people at the NCB, who thought his methods too inconsiderate of the miners' view point, nor did he believe that Peter Walker, his minister, had 'any particular regard for [him]'.

'Scargill I imagine felt a bit like Rommel had done as he swept across the desert',[24] he said, the inference being that he himself was like the victorious General Montgomery.

The cause of his greatest dissatisfaction at the beginning of the strike was the police, and he had committed himself to 'bringing about the formation of a large police force to intimidate the strikers and to exert a psychological effect upon the citizens'. At this stage he was scathing about the police,[25] largely because they had failed to 'intimidate' the pickets.

The pickets
In his respected account of 'Crowds and Power',[26] Elias Canetti describes pickets as a negative or prohibition crowd:

> There are many things which contribute to the workers' feelings of relief at the start of the strike. It is as though their hands had all dropped at exactly the same moment, and now they exert their strength not to lift them up again however hungry their families.

> But when a strike breaks out the workers equally become far more stringent. It consists then in their common refusal to continue work; and this refusal is something which permeates the whole man. The conviction created by a prohibition on work is both keen and strongly resistant.[27]

It follows that if the strike *is* to succeed every one should respect the common purpose and abide by the undertaking not to work. 'The workplace itself is forbidden ground' and pickets seek to keep it so. 'Anyone who approaches it with profane intentions, wanting to work there, is treated as an enemy or traitor'. The deeper and longer the investment of self-denial and suffering which strikers invest in their cause, the more deeply affected they are by the seeming traitoriousness of those who break the common purpose by working. The strikers know that victory for them depends on solidarity, and they also know that it is only a temporary affair, since their aim is not only to succeed in their purpose, but to return to work as soon as possible.

> As long as it remains true to its nature it [the strike] is averse to destruction. But it is true that it is not easy to keep it in this state. When things go badly and want reaches proportions difficult to bear, and if it is assailed or besieged, the negative crowd tends to revert to a positive and provocative one.[28]

Police should bear this aspect of crowd psychology in mind if they are to minimise conflict and violence. A crowd in a positive mood can retain a sufficiency of morale, but if their cause appears to be under threat there arises the prospect of destructive behaviour, and it becomes the responsibility of its leaders to call the strike off. The crowd is now no longer negative, having lost or had its original purposes frustrated, damaged or destroyed.

The picketing crowd in its negative form was well-described by a chief constable when giving evidence to a Parliamentary Select Committee (1980) in the following terms:

> One should not first of all imagine that on occasions when one has large numbers of pickets that there is a lawless situation. Quite frequently there are occasions when pickets are there in large numbers all is peaceful . . . they are sometimes there for solidarity.[29]

Where employers, non-striking workers or governments oppose the strike they have a motive for seeking to turn the crowd from its negative into its positive and more destructive form. Furthermore when the crowd becomes positive and begins to lose its pacifism, it renders itself vulnerable to destructive attacks from opposing forces such as the police, thus accelerating its defeat.

Mass secondary picketing, i.e. picketing a work place other than one's own, became a phenomenon of strikes in recent times as it was facilitated by mass motor vehicle ownership, and the modern motorway system. Organization of mass picketing was also well served by modern communications, including mobile telephones, and fax machines.

Speaking of this aspect of industrial conflict, Mrs Thatcher wrote:

> In February 1972 mass pickets led by Arthur Scargill forced the closure of the Saltley Coke Depot in Birmingham by sheer weight of numbers. It was a frightening demonstration of the impotence of the police in the face of such disorder.[30]

In the early days of the strike, Ian MacGregor was clearly agitated about what seemed to him to be a very relaxed police attitude on the picket lines; bearing in mind that his US experience at strike breaking involved the early 'formation of a large armed police force to intimidate the strikers and to exert a psychological effect upon the citizens'. Clearly the local police were not being sufficiently intimidatory and psychologically damaging at this stage, though accused of being so later on.

MacGregor was determined to see to it that the policing style should change. Although he would not be able to demand an armed police force, he would certainly be able to have a very intimidating new style riot police, able to put fear into crowds of pickets by their appearance and by the use of their offensive equipment, their horses and dogs, and *in extremis,* plastic bullets as used with such fatal consequences in Northern Ireland. He fumed: 'But it was the ill-equipped and tactically disadvantaged local police forces who were thrown into disarray that caused me most concern', and

148

in some cases they were frankly unwilling to get involved in a fight they did not see as being theirs. I was particularly concerned by reports I got that some local left-wing police committees were putting heavy pressure on their chief constables not to get involved, with the implication that the financial future of their forces could be made quite unpleasant if they were seen to be adopting the role of strike-breakers.[31]

It was quite wrong of Ian MacGregor to deride the concern of local police committees for seeking to retain adequate control of their police resources, for that is their statutory duty, but there is no doubt that some local authorities suspected his motives. In any case he wrote '. . . something clearly had to be done and soon'. He talks of 'boiling with righteous indignation', as he sought, and was quickly granted an appointment to see the prime minister and the home secretary, in that order.

He told the prime minister of his indignation over men being deprived of their freedoms and liberties through threats and intimidation, clearly referring to those miners not wishing to go on strike. As he said, it was vital to his victory that he should keep the Nottinghamshire coal mines going.

He made no bones about his contempt when he wrote '. . . it is never easy for Britons to admit that the policing of their country might be anything less than perfect—certainly a thousand times preferable to the typical American cop I was invoking to help us. I put it as vehemently as I could'. 'Prime Minister', I said, 'I am sorry to have to say this, but I never thought I would be sitting here in the UK, wishing I had a bunch of good untidy American cops out there . . .'[32]

Having told the prime minister of his preference for 'good untidy American cops' he went on further to suggest that in America the authorities would have called out the National Guard to deal with what he described as Scargill's 'well-rehearsed and organized rebellion'. Of course, as noted in *Chapter 4*, the National Guard at Kent State University had shot and killed four unarmed students, and wounded seven others during the anti-Vietnam War demonstrations of 1970. He went on:

Unhappily, I must tell you that our British police don't seem to have the same conviction about their job. This aspect of the fight is not between the NCB and the NUM. It is between men who want to work and a bunch of thugs who are trying to deprive them of that right—yet the law enforcement machinery seems to want to keep out of it.[33]

He went on to describe his delight that when speaking to the prime minister in this way he was 'preaching to the converted'. At this same meeting were present the home secretary and minister of energy, and

MacGregor recalls that after his session in the prime minister's study the National Reporting Centre at Scotland Yard was brought into life, the home secretary promised action, and within hours the situation had changed. It was after this meeting that pressure began to be put on chief constables to produce numbers of police from throughout the country with their riot equipment to begin '. . . the intimidation of the strikers', and the psychological warfare in the mining communities. There is no doubt that the Nottinghamshire coalfield (still at work) was to him 'the key to the successful solution of the dispute',[34] and the police were to be the means.

Civil or criminal
The turning of the miners strike into a year-long conflict resulted from a calculated, and somewhat ruthless tactical decision made by the National Coal Board and the government and the prime minister's personal agreement. On the miners' side, their leader, Arthur Scargill, arguably for reasons of their own aims and purposes failed to stress non-violence.

A trade dispute has, in essence, nothing to do with the police. When the government of Mrs Thatcher set about reforming the law on the trades unions in 1980, they provided civil remedies so as to keep employees and their unions under the supervision of the civil courts. The criminal law was not in issue, though—as noted—MacGregor saw the use of the police as the key force to 'intimidate the strikers and to exert a psychological effect upon the citizens'; this he managed to achieve, but at a cost to honour and decency, as well as in terms of criminalisation. Not that MacGregor can be held to blame for criminal behaviour and police excesses, but, aided by the government, he chose a path which rendered excesses inevitable.

Having suffered from mass secondary picketing (i.e. picketing at a place other than one's own workplace) at Saltley, Birmingham, in 1972, and elsewhere, the government in their Employment Act 1980 declared secondary picketing to be unlawful at civil law; this again had nothing to do with the police. The remedy in civil law is for the employer, in this case the NCB, or any other person such as a contractor, adversely affected by mass secondary picketing, to seek an injunction from a civil court to restrain such picketing. The 1980 Act also expressly removed civil immunity from other forms of picketing, and under the Employment Act 1982 removed the immunity of trade unions from civil liability completely.

The possibility of injunctions and consequent risk of unlimited fines or sequestration of assets in the event of disobedience, raised a new potent weapon in the hands of the NCB in this case. Some individuals and contractors were to use the power successfully, often encouraged and advised by MacGregor's 'war cabinet', but crucially the NCB, encouraged by the government, chose not to do so. This tactic raised important matters of principle. Lord Denning, the former Master of the Rolls, said, that '[It was] high policy at cabinet level not to use it but to call out instead, hundreds and hundreds of police'. This hit the nail on the head.[35]

MacGregor wrote, that in the first few weeks of the strike they did in fact seek an injunction for civil law remedies but decided to leave the responsibility for control of picketing to the police and the criminal law.

> In the early days we had, tentatively, gone down the route of using the government's industrial relations legislation against the miners picketing. Mr Justice Nolan granted an injunction in our favour banning flying pickets. But we never pursued the matter.[36]

He was clearly anxious not to risk alienating those trades union members who later on he wished to turn into 'scabs', and in this he was encouraged by 'leaks' from government sources about their own disquiet in using the very remedies for which they had legislated.

Arthur Scargill's biographer recounts his reaction as president of the NUM when hearing that Mr Justice Nolan had given the NCB its injunction that '. . . by invoking the legislation the Board "was setting itself in direct conflict with the National Union and all its constituent bodies" which was really legal nonsense but he was determined to wind up the politics of the strike from the very beginning'.[37]

The prime minister was kept informed of the need to keep coal moving to the power stations, and she was naturally well aware of the sensitivities of the politics of the conflict as the following passage from her memoirs shows:

> This calculation [not to pursue the injunction] had an enormous impact on our strategy. We had to act so that at any one time we did not unite against us all the other unions involved in the use and distribution of coal. This consideration meant that we all had to be very careful when and where the civil law was used, and the NCB suspended—though it did not withdraw— its civil action.[38]

Pressure now began to be exerted on the police who were to become the coercive and aggressive arm of a determined government. Early in the strike the attorney-general set before Parliament the scope of police powers to deal with mass-picketing, including the power to arrest pickets, even when leaving their own neighbourhood to travel to the picket lines; this on grounds that 'breach of the peace' may be expected. Some union officials were stopped at London's Dartford tunnel at the beginning of their 200 miles journey to the North, and lost their case on appeal. Further pressure from the chairman of the National Coal Board and the prime minister on the home secretary and the police, resulted in a speedy deployment of more than 3,000 police officers drawn from 17 police forces, and the setting up of a central coordinating agency at New Scotland Yard under the direction of the president of the Association of Chief Police Officers. Equipped as these new police formations were with riot equipment and quasi military training, they represented the most potentially aggressive police formations of all time in England. The strategy was to be a war of attrition in which the striking miners were to be beaten and diminished as a future problem once and for all. Mr MacGregor had achieved a good beginning to his purpose.

The chief constables of the various police forces are required under the Police Act 1964 to provide mutual aid when necessary and the home secretary has reserve powers to demand their collaboration.

One chief constable is recorded as saying '. . . we were seen once again in the Tonypandy role, or back to Peterloo, or even worse than that we were agents of the state'; whilst another spoke of the prime minister's fear that a secret communist cell was operating around Scargill 'to bring down the country', and that she wanted a secret police unit to be set up to counteract this. Other chief constables commented that 'MacGregor would not have been able to destroy the strike without the police' and 'I expressed the view during the miners strike that we were left in the middle of a sort of criminal law situation that should have been resolved civilly'.[39] This last comment goes to the heart of this matter.

Immense human cost resulted from this triumphant, but ethically flawed policy of the government and in addition to local policing costs; those of the reinforcements accounted for some £200 million.[40] Abandoning the civil law for the criminal law, however politically sagacious, left the police action ethically tainted.

Orgreave: A Waterloo
The most spectacular and notorious of confrontations between police and pickets took place at Orgreave coking depot in South Yorkshire between May 23 and 18 June 1984. There are numerous accounts of these events in the literature, but for present purposes their importance lies in the possibility that what was a peaceful picketing situation before this period was contrived into a violent escalation. There is evidence that this escalation was part of a strategic ploy on the part of the National Coal Board in order to relieve picketing pressure on the vital and still productive Nottinghamshire coal mines so essential to MacGregor's route to victory over the NUM.

The conflict at Orgreave reached its peak on June 18 when some 5,000 or more pickets assembled to prevent coke being transported to steel works. The pickets faced around 3,000 police officers comprising fully equipped anti-riot platoons, mounted police in protective equipment for rider and horse, and a large number of alsation police dogs.

Miners' leader, Arthur Scargill called for NUM members to '"build a picket like that at Saltley" and to come to Orgreave in such numbers that it would be impossible to move coke from the plant'.[41] Train drivers had refused to move the coke, but non-union lorry drivers were only too anxious to do so and were easily recruited by the NCB.

The volatility of the occasion produced the worst scenes of violence witnessed throughout the whole torrid year of the strike, and at the end of it the days of the miners strike were numbered.

> The violence was not confined to one side. Police officers clearly lost control of themselves, and waded into the pickets lashing out indiscriminately. Mounted police charged the crowd, and police dogs were also deployed.[42]

As MacGregor had said, it was regarded as a kind of civil war. A miner from South Wales expressed his experience in the following terms:

> Orgreave was a bloody battle ground. We left about lunch-time. We'd had a gutful. The police got out of hand. They were beating us, kicking us; the way they brought the horses in. That's why we took the bridge. It was the only way out. They had us trapped and they kept coming in and beating the shit out of us.[43]

The prime minister, Mrs Thatcher, saw such incidents from a different point of view when she said:

> The police were pelted with all kinds of missiles, including bricks and darts, and 69 people were injured. Thank goodness they had at least had proper protective riot gear.[44]

At the end of this confrontation it was reported that there had been 93 arrests. Seventy police reported injuries and 51 pickets were known to be injured, but the latter figure was regarded as a serious under-estimate. Police are required to report their injuries whilst pickets sometimes have good reason not to.[45]

A main concern about what has been called 'The Battle of Orgreave' is not so much as a kind of 'war study' but rather to determine whether or not it was engineered by the NCB to cause a diversion of pickets from the vital and still working coal mines of Nottinghamshire. There is some evidence to suggest that it was, as MacGregor explains:

Of all these efforts to divert Arthur Scargill's fire power [militarism again] the biggest, the most spectacular, and the most successful was the famous battle of Orgreave coke works.

It became a *cause célèbre* for Scargill, a fight he had to win. We were quite encouraged that he thought it so important, and did everything we could to help him continue to think so, but the truth was it mattered hardly a jot to us — beyond the fact that it kept him away from Nottingham. [46]

Kevin Hunt, the NCB's deputy director of industrial relations at the time, recalls telephoning the NUM president to say "Arthur we need more tonnage out at Orgreave". The reaction to this was "Very interesting. What do you want me to do about it?" [47]

Scargill was asked to relieve the pressure at Orgreave and this, it was said, fooled him and his friends into believing that he had an advantage over the NCB should he apply even more pressure there. This deceit which was tantamount to incitement, was further corroborated by David Hart, a pimpernel like figure who acted as a government agent, and fixer of things, to undermine the strikers as set out in the Mohawk Valley formula (see p. 133). He claimed that Orgreave was 'a set-up by us'. He is reported to have said:

> The coke was of no interest whatsoever. We didn't need it. It was a battle ground of our choosing on grounds of our choosing. I don't think Scargill believes that to this day. The fact is it was a set-up, and it worked brilliantly. [48]

If it was a 'set-up' to lure the picketing miners into conflict with the well-equipped offensive police formations, it raises important matters for principled policing. In particular it raises the principle of policing for the common good; in which case the police at Orgreave were serving the government and not the miners. The conspiracy to draw the miners into mass pickets and predictable violent conflict between the police and themselves was to depart from standards of public morality, however cunningly successful in its utilitarian character it may have been.

One answer to the Orgreave question would have been for the NCB to suspend the unnecessary Orgreave to Scunthorpe steel works coke convoys, in which case there would have been no violence, but as MacGregor said, this to him was a 'civil war', and in such matters, politically, morality is suspended.

It now remains to consider the impact which events of this kind have on police behaviour.

Police: Towards ethical corruption

The distinguished scholar of police, the late Professor Brian Chapman, was of the view that

. . . the arbitrary use of police powers, brutality, spying, secrecy, the temptation to act as a law unto itself, are characteristics inherent in every police system. They stem from the very nature of police work.

But '. . . it is a characteristic of civilised liberal democratic regimes that this potential, and the abuse is kept under control'.[49] The behaviour of police does not exist in a vacuum as we can observe when comparing and contrasting police behaviour under differing political regimes. The forces which coerce principled police behaviour include the laws, since police are subject to the same laws as everyone else, and like almost everyone else there are times when the compulsion to transgress such laws is so advantageous that they may be tempted to do so. In order to strengthen principled behaviour in police the coercion of ordinary laws is strengthened by disciplinary regulations.

If police transgressions are ignored by their colleagues and supervisors, then it is possible that such unprincipled behaviour becomes habituated. But it is not only laws and regulations in themselves which modify police behaviour for the good, but there may be found in the police an innate sense of the good, however that may arise. Among the forces which affect ethical police behaviour are awareness that their demeanour, actions, and attitudes are under public scrutiny by the press and other organized observers. Organized observers during the miners strike were the various 'Police-watch' groups. The Sheffield Police-watch Report by two women observers at Orgreave on Tuesday 29 May 1984, includes the following observation:

> We walked on towards Orgreave and Handsworth, stopping by the first house in the village above the railway. Here we observed four policemen searching the garden of the first house, which was uninhabited. They found three men in the back garden and questioned them at length about which direction they had come from. The men said they were trying to get back to their car. The policemen were aware that the conversation was being overheard, and told the men to be on their way. We feel our presence was a restraining influence on the police, and this impression was shared by a miner's wife who was also standing nearby.[50]

There is a general agreement in the reports of behaviour on the picket lines that the police were more provocative and prone to use unnecessary violence where they were numerically dominant, whereas lightly policed pickets generated less police misbehaviour. But this may not be cause and effect; light policing may only indicate anticipation of non-violent picketing. The Chesterfield observers for the National Council of Civil Liberties recorded that '. . . during the final three months of the strike when policing was much lighter, violence on the picket lines virtually disappeared'.[51]

Some police attitudes and points of view were recorded at the time in a valuable series of interviews by Roger Graef,[52] who was of the opinion that 'The year of the miners strike was to affect every officer in mainland Britain, either directly or indirectly through the tangle of moral, political and financial issues' raised by the strike. Graef likened the impact of duty on the picket lines to that of the confused moral state of some US veterans of the Vietnam War. The strike was 'a moral no-man's land' for many officers from larger urban metropolitan areas whose behaviour in these 'foreign parts' was 'another echo of Vietnam'.

A police constable, a university graduate, speaks of his 'addiction to violence' through his 'slightly awesome' role:

> . . . going up to Yorkshire for one week in four, living in an Army barracks, and working funny hours, wearing riot kit, crash helmets, regularly during the day – it becomes second nature after a while. I think you enjoy the genuine power it gives you.

Significantly for our purposes he spoke of being 'part of a vast [police] crowd, and if the whole thing is wrong [unjust?] or illegal, it's not you who is going to be picked up for it'. He found all this to be 'quite exciting' and the use of force under such circumstances to be 'quite addictive'. A colleague is recorded as by Graef as saying,

> Some bugger at the back of the crowds starts to push, and the poor sods at the front meet Mister Wood [police vernacular for being struck by batons].

The same officer said that rather than hit a man on the head because he might be killed [that would cause inquests and inquiries], 'breaking a collar-bone is best, then an elbow or a leg'. In colourful psycho speak another officer said 'If the guy is on the defensive he will start to move back. He's like an ape [sic] he starts to turn his bum on you, he is surrendering'. That's what he was taught during his training.

Innocent people were often victims of police violence and this is clearly brought out by one constable who recalled:

> Then you hit the first thing in front of you. But the first person in front of you wasn't doing anything. Legally we didn't have a leg to stand on.[53]

Setting aside those localities where throughout the strike police and pickets worked out non-violent *modus vivendi* there appear to have been times and places when the legality of picketing was not properly understood by police and pickets. Principled policing requires that protection has to be provided for pickets as well as the 'scabs' or working miners. There was considerable political pressure on the police to secure the right of miners to go to work and they showed ingenuity and determination in bringing this about; the same cannot be said about the protection of picketing rights. Where police consistently deny rights to one side in a dispute this in itself may be ethically corrupting.

Pickets alleged that the police adopted a more aggressive strategy as the strike went on.

> We [pickets] wanted to stand on the gate. They [police] wouldn't let us stand at the gate. So we tried to push our way to the gate. They brought the tall shields out . . . there were other policemen behind going over the top of the shields with their truncheons and hitting people. Then . . . dogs and horses.

Gradually, due to things going badly '. . . and want reaching proportions difficult to bear' the pickets changed from Canetti's 'negative' non-violent mood into his 'positive' or violence prone mood as frustration set in.

> Police reinforcements came running out of the transits, just shoving people back. Then a snatch squad went in and picked this youth out. They pulled him out and knocked hell out of him. Other police circled round him so you couldn't see what was happening. When they took him away there was a trail of blood from here to the van.[54]

'I saw one lad go down. This bobby had truncheoned him to the floor, unconscious . . . He'd been struck and struck until he went down, then hit again'.[55] This last witness told of knowing the number of the officer who had done this and pointing him out to the police, but they refused to note it.

> Most of them [sic] are like animals on picket lines — swinging their fists around — they're not bothered who they hit. I've been down on the picket lines and I've seen them dragging women around and ripping their coats.[56]

A woman supporter of the strike spoke of her positive attitude towards the police before the strike, but she said: 'Now I hate them. I'll never talk to a policeman again. In fact . . . when I pass a policeman in the street I cross to the other side, and my kids hate them because they took their Dad who never broke a law in his life'.[57]

Amongst a plethora of statistics concerning the strike there are some that provide clues to aspects of police practice. Of 9,808 people arrested during the strike almost 2,000 were never charged with any criminal offence; this is an indication that people were arrested often on insufficient evidence for purely perverse reasons or for convenience of the police. If this is so, then of course it indicates malpractice and a denial of rights. In addition to those who were never charged some 2,000 of those who were prosecuted were found to be not guilty, which is a very high acquittal rate for public disorder allegations.

There is one very remarkable statistic which tells its own story. A total of 1.4 million police officer days of mutual aid to local police from other forces were worked, and this averaged some 6,000 officers at any one time in addition to the thousands of local police. It is a remarkable fact that there is no record of any case at all of police officers being charged with a criminal offence, or even of being charged under the Police Discipline Regulations for 'abuse of authority'. Abuse of authority means *inter alia* to use 'unnecessary violence towards any person'.

As the strike approached its final months everyone became aware of the great demands and pressures which the police had to bear, and that at times, as the self-control of the pickets deteriorated, so the police were obliged to react with proportionate force. It became obvious that the strategy of the government and the NCB was working and the police were now being feted by government and some press. Mrs Thatcher, on one occasion, refers to them as 'our boys in blue' who had to be given all the resources that they required.

In addition to the local policing costs, those of the reinforcements from other police forces accounted for some £200 million.

Where high demands are made on the police, care has to be taken to avoid creating a feeling that they have *carte blanch* for their excesses. In a thought provoking passage, Chapman writes:

> The more that demands are made on the policeman's bravery and loyalty . . . and his instincts for order and improvement, the more he can lead himself to believe that the police are the only true moral force in society.[58]

It would be a gross exaggeration to suggest that the police took on the role of moral arbiters during the miners strike, for this would have been an indication of regression into what is sometimes called a police state, and there is no suggestion of this.

CONCLUSIONS

My main concern throughout this chapter has been to focus on the moral dimensions of the industrial dispute between government and miners, and to take note of any resulting ethical corruption of police. 'The miners strike was a blind clash of moralities', wrote Peter Jenkins, after living with a family of miners in a South Yorkshire mining village. He goes on to say:

. . . what the government called economics offended deeply against what these miners called morality. To them the moral assumptions of "Thatcherism" were utterly alien and totally repugnant. Working underground had made it self-evident to them that life was about mutual dependence.

In South Emsall people were convinced they were fighting for something much more than their pits and their livelihoods. They saw themselves as fighting for a whole way of life, a heritage which had been entrusted to them and which was not theirs to surrender'.[59]

Jenkins also noted that the prime minister never managed 'a generous word about the strikers and their families'. In his maiden speech in the House of Lords, the Earl of Stockton, former prime minister Harold Macmillan had described the miners as 'the finest body of men he'd ever known'. During what had been a trial of strength between police and pickets, policing had been characterised and influenced by a number of factors which impinged on the morality of their role:

1. The new police riot formations had been able to perform a more aggressive role than at any time in history.
2. Police in their riot formations when performing duties in other parts of the country, were not subject to the constraints which impinge on police in their own localities; within the close culture of the miners world they were more anonymous and alien.
3. Police were conscious of the steady impoverishment of the strikers and their families, whilst at the same time they were earning greatly enhanced wages, and at times were able to flaunt this.
4. Police were permanently exposed to the propaganda of those who had every political and economic reason to secure a police victory.
5. There were times, such as at Orgreave, where the management contrived to bring mass pickets and police into conflict.
6. The policing of the strike was morally flawed from the start as government and management determined that the nature of the strike should be criminalised when they chose to abandon civil law in favour of criminal justice.

It cannot be denied that the government and the NCB exercised choices which were legal and constitutional. As MacGregor said, 'management had to be allowed to manage'. It has also to be acknowledged that the miners leaders, Arthur Scargill in particular, were 'out generaled'.

Uneconomic pits were shut down, and the work force was decimated. Mining communities in most cases were economically and socially devastated. By 1993, 140 pits had been closed, and 100,000 miners forced into redundancy. The Conservative government still retained power, and the remaining mining industry was in the throes of privatisation by sale to a US company.

Endnotes

1. MacGregor, I, *The Enemies Within*, Collins: London, 1968, pp. 220-5
2. Rawls, J, *A Theory of Justice*, Oxford University Press. 1973, p. 6
3. Routledge, P, *Scargill*, Harper Collins, 1993, p. 2
4. Barrington-Moore Jnr, *Injustice: The Social Bases of Obedience and Revolt*, Macmillan: London, 1979, p. 235
5. Ibid, p. 148
6. Ibid, p. 245
7. Ibid, p. 252
8. Routledge, op. cit., p. 73
9. Whitelaw, W, *The Whitelaw Memoirs*, Headline: London, 1989, p. 161
10. Thatcher, M, *The Downing Street Years*, Harper Collins: London, 1995, p. 140
11. Home Office: 'Review of the Public Order Act, etc.': Cmnd. 7891, HMSO: London, 1982
12. 'The Brixton Disorders 10-12 April 1981', Cmnd. 8427, London, 1981, p. 66
13. Barrington-Moore Jnr, op. cit. p. 26
14. Bell, D S, *The Conservative Government*, 1979-84, Croom Helm: Beckenham, 1985, p. 2
15. Rawls, op. cit., p. 15
16. Jenkins, S, *Mrs Thatcher's Revolution*, Jonathan Cape: London, 1987
17. Winterton, J and R, *Coal, Crisis and Conflict*, Manchester University Press, 1989, p. 172
18. Ibid, p. 172-3
19. MacGregor, op. cit., p. 192
20. Ibid, p. 14
21. Winterton, 1989
22. MacGregor, op. cit., p. 151
23. Ibid, p. 185
24. Ibid, p. 190
25. Ibid, p. 191
26. Canetti, E, *Crowds and Power*, Penguin: London, 1984
27. Ibid, p. 64
28. Ibid, p. 65-66
29. Mr John Woodcock to Parliamentary Select Committee on Employment
30. Thatcher, op. cit., p. 340
31. MacGregor, op. cit., p. 191
32. Ibid, p. 191
33. Ibid, op. cit., p. 192
34. Ibid, p. 195
35. Winterton, op. cit., p. 157
36. MacGregor, op. cit., p. 216
37. Routledge, op. cit., p. 146
38. Thatcher, op. cit., p. 349
39. Reiner, R, *Chief Constables*, Oxford University Press, 1991, p. 186
40. McCabe, Wallington *et al.*, *The Police, Public Order and Civil Liberties*, Routledge: London, 1988
41. Routledge, op. cit., p. 150
42. Ibid, p. 153
43. McCabe, Wallington, *et al*, *The Public Order and Civil Liberties*, Routledge: London, 1988, p. 77

44. Thatcher, op. cit., p. 352
45. Routledge, op. cit., p. 154
46. MacGregor, op. cit., p. 205
47. Routledge, op. cit., p. 155
48. Ibid, p. 155
49. Chapman, B, *Police State,* Pall Mall: London, 1970, p. 93
50. McCabe, op. cit., p. 183
51. Ibid, p. 178
52. Graef, R, *Talking Blues*, Collins Harvill: London, 1989, p. 59
53. Ibid, p. 85
54. Gibbon, P and Steyne, D, *Thurcroft*, Spokesman: Nottingham, 1986, p. 82
55. Ibid, p. 85
56. Green, P, *The Enemy Without*, Open University Press: Milton Keynes, p. 53
57. Ibid, p. 49
58. Chapman, op. cit., p. 103
59. Jenkins, op. cit., p. 231.

CHAPTER 8

Principled Policing and the Totalitarian State

In the modern world it is not possible for the policing of totalitarian states to conform with the 'principled policing' model advanced in this book, since the two are philosophically and politically incompatible.

THE CASE OF CHINA

On 4 June 1989, after many weeks of peaceful demonstrations by university student activists and their supporters, troubled by governmental corruption and with a desire for a Chinese equivalent of Russian 'Glasnost', the People's Democratic Movement in Tiananmen Square was set upon by the Chinese People's Liberation Army, with tanks, armoured cars, and machine guns, resulting in the killing, according to various eye witness accounts, of between 1,000 and 5,000 unarmed people (statistics denied by government spokespersons). The totalitarian state had spoken in an act of callousness designed to paralyse nationwide dissent, and to serve notice on the people.

'Flying blind among mountains'
As I seek to take the reader along a fairly narrow path of the vast canvas which is the subject of China, I am conscious of the inevitable constraints upon myself, or upon anyone foolhardy enough to underestimate the subject. John King Fairbank, a foremost China scholar, warned that 'anyone who tries to understand the Chinese Revolution without a considerable knowledge of Chinese history is committed to flying blind among mountains'.[1]

China is *sui generis*—there *is* no comparison. Perhaps the nearest would have been an India which also included Pakistan. My own impressions, gained during a number of visits since the death of Mao Tse-Tung, the demise of the Gang of Four, and the end of the debacle of the Cultural Revolution, have been positive, coinciding as they have with the reforms of Deng Xiaoping. I was received most courteously by the director of the Ministry of Public Security, being the first official police visitor from the West since China had become more open under Deng Xiaoping.

Western liberal though I may be, it did not deter senior police officials from seeking my professional opinions on the situation. At the end of my first visit in 1980 during my de-briefing by government officials from the Ministry of Public Security, the senior officer commanded 'Alderson criticise!', which I did, advocating studies of policing and criminology and the setting up of appropriate institutes—and these have long since been undertaken. So, my own view, critical though it may be at times, is one of understanding of the immense responsibility for maintaining a peaceful social order in China whilst advancing reforms. Too much too soon may lead to disaster, too little too late even more so.

As we turn to take note of relevant facts, consequences, and criticisms, I do so with an abundance of goodwill towards the Chinese people.

The issues arising from the 1989 protest movement in China culminating in the Tiananmen Square debacle are of great importance to the world order. As one commentator put it, 'Once people have dared to fight back, no dictatorship can ever be sure of its power again. In that respect, if no other, the protest in Tiananmen Square was the beginning of the end of the communist party rule in China'.[2] But can this be true of a China becoming richer and more powerful by the day; the world's greatest state governed by an authoritarian system with the backing of a powerful military machine? We must not forget China's long tradition of hierarchical government, and that fragmentation of the social order may once more signal the re-emergence of 'warlordism' which is not a prospect favoured by the vast majority of the Chinese people.

So let us take note of a few details which may help us with our understanding of the vast and complex state which, governed under the political philosophy of 'democratic centralism' requires a police system commensurate with its historical, social, cultural and political complexities.

Figures and facts

The estimated population of China (1992) is some 1,171 millions; around six per cent of whom belong to 55 ethnic minorities. China is a unitary state. Directly under the central government there are 22 provinces, five autonomous regions, including Tibet, and the three municipalities, (Beijing, Shanghai, and Tianjin).

The principal language in Northern China is Mandarin and its dialectal versions. The Tibetans, Uyurs, Mongols, and other groups have their own languages.

In addition to Confucianism, Buddhism, and Daoism, there are Muslim and Christian minorities.

Stretching from Russia in the north, to India and Burma in the south, China is vast (3,705,408 square miles).

As already noted, the political traditions of China have a lengthy and complex history, but it is now necessary for present purposes to examine them a little closer.

Totalitarianism and Chinese traditions

In the political vocabulary, the term totalitarianism is comparatively new, though political systems which it describes are quite ancient. Both Confucious (Kung Fu-tzu: c.500 BC) and his western near contemporary, Plato (c.428-328) favoured political systems which were totalitarian in nature and design. 'In Confucian philosophy government has to be the function of a specialist ruling group'.[3]

> So government for the people and in consultation with the people was a basic Confucious ideal, but the further step of government by the people was never an issue in traditional China.[4]

Confucious would find modern China, at least in this regard, very much in line with his own thinking. People have distinct roles, which they must perform for the sake of the orderly arrangement of society; in Confucious's words:

> Let the prince be the prince, the minister the minister, the father the father, and the son a son.[5]

And *we* might add:

> ... the Politburo the Politburo.

Plato advanced similar ideas in his *Republic*. Popper writes that 'Plato's political programme, far from being morally superior to totalitarianism, is fundamentally identical with it'.[6] Neither Confucious nor Plato envisaged room for change in their versions of the social order, any more than the Chinese Communist Party does today. Plato decried democracy, and despised democrats of his time.[7]

Plato's social order was immutable, being made up of three classes, namely the guardians, the auxiliaries or warriors (police and soldiers) and the working class. In the Confucian state 'a hierarchical society is essential to the achievement of political order', and throughout Imperial Chinese history officials, whether active or retired, enjoyed a very privileged position in matters of law, since it was deemed sufficient for a man's honour to control his conduct.

This idea of rule by men of honour continued right up to the twentieth century ensuring that 'the Rule of Law' has no great place in Chinese history. The criminal justice system, such as it was, was regarded with hostility as '. . . the harshness of the state's legal processes was exacerbated by the extortionist behaviour of the police'.[8]

There appears to be no tradition in Chinese history which would militate unduly against rule by officials and their dictatorship. Individual freedom does not seem to have been a concept which raised its head in any significant form, and is often viewed as a dangerous liberal tendency threatening the social order.

Modern totalitarianism defined

The twentieth century has been witness to many totalitarian regimes both of the political left and right—and in every case it is the power of the police that is a distinctive outstanding feature. Given appropriate circumstances, totalitarianism has shown itself capable of germinating even so-called 'advanced societies'. For our present purposes we need to define its modern characteristics, and to do that I propose to use the definition supplied by Karl Dietrich Bracher.[9]

I will take pieces of the Bracher definition and then an appropriate and relevant article from the Constitution of the People's Republic of China, 1982 (amended in 1993).

> *Bracher:* Fundamental to all totalitarian regimes is the claim to exclusive leadership.

> *Article 1:* The People's Republic of China is a socialist state under the people's democratic dictatorship led by the working class and based on the alliance of workers and peasants. Sabotage of the socialist system by any organization or individual is prohibited.

> *Bracher:* Rival political parties or groups are precluded, and fundamental claims to individual liberty and civil rights are denied.

> *Article 51:* The exercise by citizens of the People's Republic of China of their freedoms and rights may not infringe upon the interests of the state, of society, and of the collective.

> *Bracher:* Therefore, it's pseudo-democratic legitimisation notwithstanding, totalitarianism is a fundamental contradiction of the democratic creed of human rights, whether it denies them explicitly or undermines them by manipulation.

> *Article 2:* All power in the People's Republic of China belongs to the people. [The 'people' are not defined, nor does the Constitution acknowledge the right of people to canvas political movements; in fact it specifically denies

it—author's comment].

Article 3: The state organs of the People's Republic of China apply the principle of democratic centralism. [The cynic might say 'all centralism and no democracy'—author's comment]

Democratic centralism: Diverges from what it purports to be. Its real utility is to free communist leaders from accountability to party members . . . decision making is jealously guarded as the exclusive preserve of self-selected, unaccountable ruling groups . . . in practice centralism; the democratic aspect is cosmetic and ascriptive.[10]

Article 57: The National People's Congress of the People's Republic of China is the highest organ of state power. [All deputies are elected by the Communist Party].

China's Confucian heritage, which is still culturally strong, is not in conflict with the communist political system, but as in modern times ideas are carried through international mass communication, there is likely to be conflict, even violent conflict, from time to time, and undoubtedly crushing blows will then be delivered through the People's Liberation Army or the People's Police, and particularly through the use of secret police, clandestine incarceration, and executions. There is much at stake in maintaining public order in China.

The People's Armed Police
At present there are about 530,000 members of the PAP, stationed at national, regional and local level; their duties are to guard frontiers and internal utilities and to assist in maintaining public order. Its nearest European equivalent would be the French Gendarmerie, the Spanish Guarda Civile, and the Italian Carabinieri; they are soldiers carrying out civil policing functions and while basically under the Central Military Commission of the government, for policing functions they answer to the Ministry of Public Security. In 1989, the PAP was neither organized, trained or led with sufficient purpose to deal with the Democratic Movement's protest, and this was the main reason why the PLA was eventually committed to its murderous tactics.

'The People's Police Cherishes the People'
Slogans are commonplace in Chinese lore, probably due to the Confucian tradition, and the above police slogan is part of current propaganda. One is reminded of George Orwell's brilliant parody of the totalitarian state in his novel, *Nineteen-Eighty-Four*, where law and order is the responsibility of the Ministry of Love.

Principled Policing

There are 1.6 million police officers in China, and their duties are set out by the Ministry of Public Security in the following notes. These are an English translation of the Ministry of Public Security's description, but edited for present purposes.:

Chinese Police Agencies their Duties and Functions
The People's Police agencies are composed of the Ministry of Public Security, with local public security organs at various levels.

1. Ministry of Public Security of the state is the equivalent of Interior Ministries, or Home Departments in western states.
2. Provincial Public Security agencies (22) exercise delegated authority in China's provinces.
3. Autonomous regions (5), though having their own regional government, are nevertheless not autonomous, but delegated, in matters of public security.
4. Municipalities (3) Beijing, Shanghai, and Tienjin have the same public security powers as the Regions.
5. At the micro-level there are Local People's Congresses with their local responsibilities for public security departments. [The Confucian tradition is very strong in recognising the place of the extended family, collectives, and communes, as being the primary cells of government].

The principal police duties include:
1. To guard against and deal blows at the acts of sabotage of the counter-revolutionaries. [That this should be the primary duty of police of China is indicative of the concern of the Communist Party to secure its monopoly of power. The phrase 'to deal blows' is obviously not a legal phrase, but one which might suggest some form of political thuggery].
2. To guard against and deal blows at all kinds of crimes, including economic crimes. [The stressing of economic crimes is commensurate with the political philosophy of 'the socialist state', though the many radical economic reforms introduced since 1978 by Deng Xiaoping are still working their largely successful way through China's buoyant economy, whilst all the time weakening the ties of pure Marxist–Leninist–Maoist communism].
3. To engage in administrative duties for maintaining public order, including residents registration, traffic regulation and fire fighting. [I will consider the failure of the police to maintain public order in Tiananmen Square in 1989 in due course].
4. To administer foreigners entering and leaving the country.
5. To do guard duty.
6. To arrest or detain suspects by law and carry out preliminary questioning and detention.
7. To do other duties assigned by the government. [This last duty is typical of policing in totalitarian states since it implies that policing when extended by government decree may not be subject to the Rule of Law].

167

In addition to the Ministry of Public Security, there is the Ministry of State security which deals with secret and political police concerns including taking action against 'enemies of the people' and foreign subversion.

Now I must turn to consider the dominant place of the People's Liberation Army in the China of today and why what happened in Beijing in 1989 happened as it did.

'The People's Liberation Army men are like fish in the sea of the people' (Mao Tse Tung)

The People's Liberation Army in its short history—1927 to the present— occupies a special place in the triumph of the 'people' over the 'running dogs' of Western capitalism, the Kuomintang, which is now practising a style of democracy in Taiwan. Until recent times the PLA dominated the ranks of Chinese Communist Party government; in 1969 its representation on the Politburo and Central Committee stood at 50 per cent.

Having defeated its internal foe, the Kuomintang, and seen the Japanese invaders sent packing from occupied Manchuria, its other great strength lay in its involvement in the reconstruction and development of agriculture and industry. The production brigades which under Mao Tse Tung applied their military discipline to the workplace, saw to it that performances were raised in line with government directives. In his selected works Mao's Confucian-style aphorisms concerning the PLA include:

> Every communist must grasp the truth "political power grows out of the barrel of a gun".

> Our principle is that the Party controls the gun, and the gun must never be allowed to command the Party.[11]

PLA and the Constitution

Article 29 of the 1982 Constitution of the Chinese People's Republic provides:

> The Armed Forces of the People's Republic of China belong to the people. Their tasks are to strengthen national defence, resist aggression, safeguard the people's peaceful labour, participate in the national reconstruction, and work hard to serve the people.

There are sufficient ambiguities and loopholes in the above article which, when allied with other articles, e.g. article 1, 'Sabotage of the socialist system by any organization or individual is prohibited', may be used to justify use of the Armed Forces against internal disorder.

168

Principled Policing

It is pertinent to note that 'according to the Chinese government's own statistics, 70 per cent of reported economic crimes during 1987-1988 were committed by officials, including officers and other ranks of the PLA'.

At the Gate of the Heavenly Peace

The Gate of the Heavenly Peace in Beijing is that entrance to the Forbidden City of Imperial China above which hangs the massive portrait of Chairman Mao; the Gate also faces Tiananmen square.

The square is an awesome sight; intimidating by its scale. I still remember the pervading Orwellian atmosphere of the place with the great portraits of Marx, Engels, Lenin, and Stalin, ten storeys high (but now removed), and platoons of workers, in the Maoist uniformed clothing of the time, jogging along to their labours. It is a vast area in which great dramas could be enacted by millions of people, and in 1989 it became a theatre in which the players on the one hand were vulnerable members of the Democracy Movement, and on the other, the powerful armed battalions of the People's Liberation Army.

The Democracy Movement

Conceived in fury and consumed by fire, the 1989 Democracy Movement is a watershed in the history of China and the communist world.[12]

It is not our purpose to go into great detail about the origin, growth, and defeat of the Democracy Movement, but to express it only in brief and general terms. We might note that the totalitarian state is always vulnerable when the air is pervaded by the desire for reform. The reforms being demanded by the Democracy Movement would not be seen to be exceptional in a democratic society. They were as follows:

1. To clear the name of Hu Yaobang. [Hu Yaobang was General Secretary of the Communist Party and widely regarded as a man who wanted to create a freer political system. Deng forced him to resign and this was regarded by the Democracy Movement as an injustice—he died from a heart attack during a Politburo meeting]
2. To repudiate the campaigns which had been waged against bourgeois liberalisation and spiritual pollution.
3. To publish details about the assets and incomes of party leaders and their relatives.
4. To allow freedom of speech and of free press.
5. To increase funding on further education.
6. To raise the salaries of teachers and other intellectuals; and
7. To lift all restrictions on street demonstrations.

169

It is the general view that the Deng Xiaoping reforms, beginning in 1979, sought to change and to liberate the economy without at the same time reforming and liberating the politics, with the inevitable resulting tensions. It is well known that plentiful supplies of the basic needs of human life, of food, of shelter, clothing, warmth, security, and creature comforts, tend to cause minds to think of higher things such as education, information and ultimately freedom.

The movement began to develop at a faster pace in 1989. May 4 was the seventieth anniversary of an earlier student's protest for change from Imperial China to a Republic. Now both members of faculties and students were gaining resolve to demonstrate for change once again. It is reported that the leaders of the Communist Party were uneasy about this. Wall posters appeared, and demonstration marches of protest took place, even a plaster copy of the Statue of Liberty was erected in defiance. The death of the most popular politician, Hu Yaobong, only served to increase emotions which generated more dynamism for political protest against the *status quo*.

The police were fairly passive, and law enforcement was undoubtedly difficult, but above all the police had not been adequately trained and suitably equipped to deal with protest movements with adequate force. The danger now was the obvious gulf between ordinary uniformed police detachments and 'military aid to the civil power' as we would call it in England. Force was to be either inadequate, or deadly, to deal with what government sources were ominously beginning to describe as 'counter-revolutionaries', a treasonable and subversive category.

The many demands for political reform, an end to official corruption and nepotism, which always flourish under conditions of dictatorship, and more open government, were among those reforms demanding an answer from within the bureaucratic system housed in the government buildings of the hierarchy. Initially the police made no attempt to move the crowds which grew both in numbers and in confidence. Later police loudspeakers began to call for the dispersal of the protesters, and when they failed to disperse 'hundreds of police swarmed' around them and many did disperse. Meanwhile protests around the country were growing.

Deng Xiaoping is reported as demanding stiffer action against what he called, 'the conspiracy to negate the leadership of the Communist Party and the socialist system'.[13]

Reading accounts of this period reveals a situation calling for a mixture of firmness, understanding, and tolerance, but, as Deng put it, 'we have several million People's Liberation Army soldiers. What are we afraid of?'

The student protesters meanwhile published lists of the details of their charges of nepotism and corruption among the ranks of the top officials of the Communist Party. Party officials countered with threats of a 'clear cut response', published in the official organ, the *People's Daily*.

The PLA were ordered to station large forces of troops on the periphery of Beijing. On April 27, a defiant reply came from the protesters in the form of a parade some 150,000 strong, and the government offered a 'parley'. Throughout, the protests there were a number of parleys between leading activists and government officials but they failed to bear much fruit.

The visit, however, of the Russian prime minister, Mikhail Gorbachev, from May 15 to 18 also took place during the protest, much to the embarrassment—and therefore serious loss of face of—the Communist party. The staging of a hunger strike by 1,000 volunteers in the square was another powerful blow which brought out a senior party official to express both sympathy and admonition.

'Power Grows out of the Barrel of a Gun' (Mao Tse Tung).

On Saturday May 20, Li Peng the prime minister, announced that martial law would now take effect, and more troops were assembled.[14] Apparently there is no definition of martial law in Chinese law, but its ordinary meaning in international understanding is the suspension of ordinary laws and control through military decree. Some countries, including the UK, legislate for emergency powers under these circumstances in order to preserve the Rule of Law. The effect of the government measures in China seems to have brought an angry response from the people and support for the student protesters. The escalation towards some degree of violence was now foreshadowed if the stalemate between protesters' intransigence and government transfixity was to be resolved.

The situation was reminscent of Paris in 1795 during the French Revolution when Napoleon Bonaparte, facing the insurgents in the Rue Saint Honore issued his famous order to shoot them down—*pour encourager les autres,* it is said. In less than a day, Napoleon had subdued a serious Royalist uprising and thereby saved the Republic. The Chinese government were looking for a Napoleon.

Demonstrations throughout China waxed and waned

Public protest was now beginning to manifest itself throughout the People's Republic, no doubt adding to the party's apprehension of losing power on the one hand or of using it on the other.

A week into the movement, the number of cities which had rallies and demonstrations swelled to 12 with a total reported mobilisation making a

171

record high of over 400,000 people on April 22. [15]

A second peak was reached when over 200,000 students from 42 Beijing colleges converged on Tiananmen Square, breaking police picket lines and, it is said, attracting over a million Beijing residents en route. On May 4, a second surge of protests took place on the seventieth anniversary of an earlier student demonstration. This time 29 cities mobilised more than a million participants.

From May 14 to 23 a succession of happenings kept protest 'on the boil'. Dialogue between students and government leaders, Gorbachev's visit, the high profile hunger strike of hundreds of students, the confrontation by Beijing residents with martial law troops signalled growing popular support for the protesting students, all adding further dimensions to the drama. By June, 132 cities had participated in the protests; the dragon was twitching its tail.[16]

Policing failure

The police failure was not in failing to facilitate protest so much as to bring about its dispersal with minimum casualties. This was due to a combination of a lack of preparedness for the event and professional incompetence. Chairman Deng and his senior comrades were seeking to play an astute role meanwhile. The secret police were of course very active, and the list of 'most wanted' persons was growing daily.

It is recorded that, by June 4, the military forces around Beijing numbered some 250,000. There were those amongst retired PLA marshalls opposed to taking over the police role by the use of troops and their fire power. The use of unarmed junior soldiers as a deterrent had resulted in their being humiliated and taunted by ranks of Beijing residents.

The military prepares

As Michael Byrnes said,

> . . . after weeks of being subject to a strict news blackout, and being thoroughly "briefed" by their political commissars on the unlawful counter-revolutionary activities of the demonstrators, the PLA used the techniques, that as a military force it was trained for, shooting the "enemy".

But 'the PLA was ordered to attack the objective it was created to defend—the people'.[17] The *Liberation Army News,* was quick to ensure that the troops knew where their loyalty lay:

> At any time, under any circumstances, we must firmly maintain the
> principle that the Party commands the gun. The Army must be subject to
> the Party's absolute leadership. The Army is a proletarian military force
> created and led by the Chinese Communist Party, and is an armed group
> for carrying out the Party's political tasks.[18]

This is a classic example of totalitarianism. Though called the 'People's
Army', in reality it was the Communist Party's Army, and this provides
another example of Orwellian 'newspeak'.

A government paper given to the author stressed that 'This turmoil
was not a chance occurrence. It was a political turmoil incited by a very
small number of political careerists . . . aimed at subverting the People's
Republic'. It also spoke of dissension within the Party's hierarchy,
between the Conservatists and the Reformists. 'Foreign sources' (largely
meaning Western, particularly US) were accused of fabricating rumours.
'Violent rebellion' was abroad in an attempt to 'overthrow the
government and seize power at one stroke'; hardly a possibility when
considering the disparity of power between dissidents and the PLA, as
Deng knew only too well, for he was chairman of the Military
Commission.

Denouement

The former British Ambassador in Beijiing, Sir Richard Evans writes:

> The army entered Peking in massive strength during the night of 3-4 June.
> Several hundred civilians at least were killed and thousands wounded as
> columns of tanks, armoured personnel carriers, and lorries carrying armed
> men and much equipment forced their way towards the centre of the city
> from points all around its periphery.[19]

He goes on to describe the killing of people by the Army including the
killing of women and children, office and factory workers, and
professional people, many of whom were shot down on the barricades
and many as they fled down side streets.

Quite a few soldiers were killed as well as members of the People's
Armed Police. He found it impossible to make sense of official figures
which did not tally with the facts, but in any case they were used to
underpin political points.

The shooting down of unarmed civilians continued throughout
two nights and a day. Eye witness accounts and journalists' reports
served to confirm the considerable brutality of the PLA. 'Scores of
people standing under a row of trees or sitting on benches were
sprayed with bullets'.

173

Hundreds of troops crouched behind concrete blocks . . . For one endless minute the bullets poured out. As bodies crumpled to the ground the crowd behind them scattered. The soldiers were riding armoured vehicles and used their machine guns against thousands of local residents. [20]

The Radio Peking (English Language) Service surprisingly broadcast the following remarks: 'Among the dead are colleagues at Radio Peking'; and 'Ordinary people were stunned by the army's savagery'.[21]

Aftermath
After the Tiananmen Square protest for democratic reform of China's totalitarian state had been put down by the PLA with such deadly consequences, the Democracy Movement went quiet, the people went home, and the leaders either fled abroad or were incarcerated in one of China's Ministry of State Security 'gulags'. The People's Police no doubt went back to their stations and barracks wondering what it was that had overtaken them.

CONCLUSIONS

I began this chapter by proffering the hypothesis that the model for principled policing advanced in this book was both philosophically and politically incompatible with the totalitarian state.

That our model should prove to be incompatible with policing methods of the Chinese People's Republic is of fundamental importance to its worth. Events surrounding protests by the Democracy Movement for greater political freedom in the period leading up to the Tiananmen massacre by the PLA in June 1989 were a vindication of the value of our model for justice and for freedom. It would however have produced a remarkable situation had principled policing been implanted into the Chinese system, for then the logical and resulting outcome would have been the People's Police arresting and charging members of the PLA!

The theory of protectionism set out earlier would have required the People's Police to protect the citizens from injustices by the state, as well as protecting their freedoms, including the freedom to protest peacefully. Under the social contract theory, which we now know cannot function in a totalitarian state, those freedoms being protected were those which did not harm the freedoms of other people.

We should also take note, and remind ourselves of those impediments to principled policing which arises from the Constitution of the PRC. Article 51 of the Constitution permits 'the interests of the state' (not restricted by definition) to be invoked by the state against those individual and collective rights which it purports to protect. Thus it is that police are not able to protect any so-called 'rights' which the state, i.e. the Communist Party, declares to be an infringement of the 'state interest', whatever that may be.

An additional obstruction to principled policing in the PRC is the lack of a developed concept of the Rule of Law, in the absence of which legal objectivity associated with principled policing is not enabled, at least to some degree, to evolve. Not being influenced and guided by a well entrenched theory of the Rule of Law would render the People's Police subject to the exigencies of political caprice.

It seems therefore that the arbiter of what principles should determine the role of the police in the PRC, at any point in time, would not be a democratic one, as we in the West understand it, since the decision would fall to the State Council. The State Council is the highest institution of state power and administration; it is a self-elected body appointed by the hierarchy of the Communist Party.

And so we are right to conclude that our theory of 'principled policing' is incompatible with the concept of totalitarianism.

Endnotes

1. Fairbank, J K, *The Great Chinese Revolution: 1800-1985*, Picador/Pan Books: London, 1988, p. 11
2. Buruma, I, *New York Review of Books*, vol. XLII, No. 20. p. 9
3. Dawson, R D, *Confucius*, Oxford University Press: Oxford, 1981, p. 66
4. Ibid, p. 64
5. Ibid, p. 66
6. Popper, K R, *The Open Society and Its Enemies*, Routledge: London, 1989, p. 87
7. Ibid, p. 41/42
8. Dawson, op. cit., p. 72/73
9. Bracher, K D, *The Blackwell Encyclopaedia of Political Science*, Blackwell: Oxford, 1991, p. 614
10. Ibid, p. 169
11. Mao Tse Tung, 'Quotations', Second Edition, Foreign Language Press: Peking, 1967, p. 61 and p. 102
12. Tong, J, *The 1989 Democracy Movement in China*, South East Asia Studies: Hong Kong University, 1994, p. 2
13. Fathers, M and Higgins, A, *Tiananmen: The Rape of Peking*, Transworld: London, 1989, p. 32 and 34 *et seq.*
14. Ibid, pp. 51 and 60
15. Ibid, p. 79
16. Tong, op. cit., p. 5
17. Byrnes, M, 'The Death of a People's Army' in *The Broken Mirror*, Longmans: London, 1990, p. 141
18. Ibid, p. 145

19. Evans, R, *Deng Xiaoping and The Making of Modern China*, Penguin Books: London, 1995, p. 296
20. Fathers, op. cit., p. 126
21. Ibid, p. 127.

Postscript

As we turn to close this discourse there is a need to be reminded that what I have sought to achieve is the provision of a moral philosophical foundation for the policing of liberal democratic societies.

Principled policing is not the same thing as *principles of police science* which, where functioning without a moral basis as at times they do, pose a potential threat to the humanitarianism of the policing function. Examples of policing have been provided which—by design or by accident—are detached from a principle of morality. We have discovered principles which, if adhered to, should offer protection for Human Rights, which may otherwise be denied by unfettered police science, the pursuit of unprincipled dogma, and an absence of or weaknesses in, the theory of the Rule of Law.

We have been faced with the shift of modern philosophy of government from the dominance of utilitarianism towards that of human rights. In the words of L H A Hart:

> We are currently witnessing . . . the progress of a transition from a once widely accepted old faith that some form of utilitarianism . . . must capture the essence of political morality.

> Whereas not so long ago great energy and much ingenuity of many philosophers were devoted to making some form of utilitarianism work, latterly such energies and ingenuity have been devoted to the articulation of theories of basic rights.[1]

It is a stark uncomfortable truth that the Europe of The Enlightenment, the cradle of Parliamentary democracy, is the same Europe which has inflicted the most outrageous behaviour upon people in and out of war, and now through insistence upon the priority of human rights seeks to gain some self respect.

Following upon the Second World War it is no longer a question of national choice whether to grant or deny rights, but a matter for provisions of international law stemming from the Universal Declaration of Human Rights of 1948. It is for these reasons that policing internationally has to discover essential moral principles with which to discharge its obligations in upholding Human Rights as I have tried to illustrate in the foregoing chapters. It is to the theory of the social contract that we have looked for a rationale which justifies Lycophron's idea that 'The law is a convenant by which men assure one another of justice', and that the state represents 'a cooperative

177

association for the prevention of crime'. Together these principles amount to the theory of 'protectionism' which I described in *Chapter 1*. The rights being protected are those which 'do not harm other citizens', and their protection has to be equal yet individual and always 'against injustice'.

It is not a contradiction of this theory to describe it as being towards 'the common good' since if it is for the good of each individual equally then it is a good held in common, and the police are amongst its trustees.

Thus it is that the theories of principled policing outlined in this work are able to advance and protect the moral good of society as the modern philosophy of government strives to secure the primacy of Human Rights.

Endnote

1 Ryan, A (Ed.), *The Idea of Freedom,* Oxford University Press, 1979, p. 77

Bibliography

Alderson, J C, *Policing Freedom*, Macdonald and Evans: Plymouth, 1979

Alderson, J C, *Human Rights and the Police*, Council of Europe: Strasbourg, 1984

Alderson, J C, *Law and Disorder*, Hamish Hamilton: London, 1984

Alderson, J C. and Stead, PJ (eds), *The Police We Deserve*, Wolfe: London, 1973

Arendt, H, *Eichmann in Jerusalem*, Penguin: London, 1994

Ayer, A J, *The Central Questions of Philosophy*, Penguin: London, 1976

Benyon, J, (ed.), *Scarman and After*, Pergamon Press: London, 1984

Bishop and Mallie, *The Provisional IRA*, Corgi: London, 1988

Boucher and Kelly, (eds), *The Social Contract from Hobbes to Rawls*, Routledge: London, 1994

Browder, G C, *Hitler's Enforcers*, Oxford University Press: New York, 1990

Browning, C R, *Ordinary Men*, Harper Collins: New York, 1992

Bruce, S, *The Red's Hand*, Oxford University Press: Oxford, 1992

Buckland, P, *History of Northern Ireland*, Gill and Macmillan: Dublin, 1981

Bullock, A, *Hitler – A Study in Tyranny*, Penguin: London, 1962

Byrnes, M, 'The Death of a People's Army' in *The Broken Mirror*, Longmans: London, 1990

Cameron, The Hon, Lord, DSC, *Disturbances in Northern Ireland*, Report of Commission, Cmnd. 532, HMSO: London, 1969

Canetti, E, *Crowds and Power*, Penguin: London, 1973

Chapman, B, *Police State*, Macmillan: London, 1971

Clausewitz, C von, *On War*, Penguin: London, 1968

Clutterbuck, R, *Protest and the Urban Guerrilla*, Cassells: London, 1973

Clutterbuck, R, *Britain in Agony*, Faber and Faber: London, 1978

Coogan, T P, *The IRA*, Fontana: London, 1980

Cowel, Jones and Young, *Policing the Riots*, Junction Books: London, 1982

Crick, M, *Scargill and The Miners*, Penguin: London, 1985

Dawson, R D, *Confucius*, Oxford University Press: Oxford, 1981

Dhillon, K S, *Defenders of the Establishment*, Indian Institute of Advanced Study, Shimla, 1998

Dworkin, R, *Taking Rights Seriously*, Duckworth: London, 1977

Evans, R, *Deng Xiaoping and the Making of Modern China*, Penguin Books: London, 1995

Eveleigh, R, *Peace Keeping in a Democratic Society*, Hurst: London, 1978

Ewing and Gearty, *Freedom Under Thatcher*, Oxford University Press: Oxford, 1990

Fairbank, J K, *The Great Chinese Revolution – 1800-1885*, Picador/Pan Books, London: 1988

Fathers, M and Higgins, A, *Tiananmen:The Rape of Peking*, Transworld: London, 1989

Finer, S E, (ed.), *Five Constitutions*, Penguin: London, 1979

Fosdick, R, *European Police Systems*, The Century Company: New York, 1915

Geary, R, *Policing Industrial Disputes*, Methuen: London, 1986

Gellner, E, *Conditions of Liberty*, Hamish Hamilton: London, 1994

Gentry, C, *J. Edgar Hoover*, Norton: New York, 1991

Graef, R, *Talking Blues*, Collins Harvill, 1989

Green, P, *The Enemy Without: Policy and Class Consciousness in the Miner's Strike* Open University Press: Buckingham, 1990

Guyer, P, Ed. *Kant: Cambridge Companion*, Cambridge University Press: Cambridge, 1992

Haggard, P, *Police Ethics*, Edwin Mellon Press: Lampeter, 1994

Hamill, D, *Pig in the Middle*, Methuen: London, 1985

Hare, R M, *Moral Thinking*, Oxford University Press: Oxford, 1981

Harris, K, *Thatcher*, Weidenfeld and Nicholson: London, 1987

Herring, G C, *America's Longest War*, Second Edition, McGraw Hill: New York, 1986

Hohne, H, *The Order of the Death's Head*, Pan: London, 1986, 1972

Hudson, W D, *Modern Moral Philosophy*, 2nd Edition: Macmillan: London, 1983

Kant, I, *The Metaphysical Elements of Justice*, John Ladd: trans. Bobbs-Merrill: New York, 1965

Karnow, S, *Vietnam: A History*, Penguin: London, 1984

Kee, R, *Ireland: A History*, Abacus: London, 1982

Kerner Report, 'President's Advisory Committee on Civil Disorders', Bantam: New York, 1968

Khrushchev, N, *Khrushchev Remembers*, Deutsch: London, 1971

Knight, A, *Beria: Stalin's First Lieutenant*, Princeton University: Princeton, 1993

Kohel, R L, *The Black Corps*, University of Wisconsin Press, 1983

Lessnoff, M, *Social Contract Theory*, Blackwell: Oxford, 1990

Locke, J, *The Second Treatise on Government*, Prometheus: New York, 1986

MacGregor, I, *The Enemies Within*, Collins: London, 1986

Mackenzie, *Power, Violence and Decision*, Penguin: London, 1975

Maine, Sir H, *Ancient Law*, Dent: London, 1917

Mao tse-Tung, *Quotations* ('The Little Red Book'), Foreign Language Press: Peking, 1967

McCabe, Wallington *et. al.*, *The Police, Public Order and Civil Liberties*, Routledge: London, 1988

McNamara, R, with B Van Der Mark, *In Retrospect: The Tragedy and Lessons of Vietnam*, Times Books: New York, 1995

McNee, Sir D, *McNee's Law*, Collins: London, 1983

Murdoch, I, *Metaphysics as a Guide to Morals*, Chatto and Windus: London, 1992

Northam, G, *Shooting in the Dark*, Faber and Faber: London, 1988

Ottey, R, *The Strike*, Sidgwick and Jackson: London, 1985

Padfield, P, *Himmler*, Papermac: London, 1990

'People of Thurcroft, Thurcroft: A Village and the Miners Strike', Spokesman: Nottingham, 1986

Popper, K R, *The Open Society and Its Enemies*, Routledge: London, 1989

Popper, K R, *The Poverty of Historicism*, Routledge: London, 1991

Pryce, K, *Endless Pressure*, Penguin: London, 1979

180

Rawls, J, *The Theory of Justice*, Oxford University Press: Oxford, 1973

Rawls, J, *Justice as Fairness*, Oxford University Press: Oxford, 1973

Rawls, J, *Political Liberalism*, Columbia University Press: New York, 1993

Reiner, R, *Chief Constables*, Oxford University Press: Oxford, 1991

Rousseau, J, *The Social Contract and Discourses*, Dent: London, 1986

Routledge, P, *Scargill*, Harper Collins: London, 1993

Russell, B, *History of Western Philosophy*, 2nd Edition, Allen and Unwin: London, 1961

Ryder, C, *The RUC*, Methuen: London, 1989

Sabine, G H, *A History of Political Theory*, 3rd Edition, Harrap: London, 1963

Sakharov, A, *Memoirs*, Hutchinson: London, 1990

Scarman, Mr Justice, 'Report of Tribunal of Inquiry on Violence and Civil Disturbances in Northern Ireland in 1969', Cmd. 566. HMSO: London, 1972

Scarman, Mr Justice, 'The Brixton Disorders 10-12 April 1981', HMSO: Cmnd. 8427, 1981

Seanor and Fotion, *Hare and Critics*, Clarenden Press: Oxford, 1988

Stone, I F, 'The Killings at Kent State', *New York Review,* 1970

Taylor, D (ed.), *The Troubles*, Macdonald, Thames: London, 1980

Thatcher, M, *The Downing Street Years*, Harper Collins: London, 1995

Wells, J M (Ed.), *The People vs. Providential War,* Dunellen: New York, 1970

Whitelaw, W, *The Whitelaw Memoirs*, Headline: London, 1990

Whyte, J, *Interpreting Northern Ireland*, Clarendon: Oxford, 1991

Wiesenthal, S, *Justice Not Vengeance*, Widenfeld and Nicholson: London, 1989

Widgery, The Rt. Hon. Lord, 'Report of Tribunal on Events of Sunday 30 January 1972 in Londonderry', HMSO: London, HL101, HC220

Williams, B, Morality: *An Introduction to Ethics*, Cambridge University Press: Cambridge, 1972

Winterton, J and R, *Coal, Crisis and Conflict*, Manchester University Press: Manchester, 1990

Index

A selection of other titles from Waterside Press

📖 **The Prisons Handbook** Mark Leech A major work. The definitive guide to penal establishments in England and Wales listing addresses, telephone and fax numbers, Internet sites, personnel - and containing a wealth of detailed information about prisons and imprisonment. An invaluable resource for anyone needing to deal with prisons on a regular basis. *A tour de force: Prison Service Journal.* (1998) ISBN 1 872 870 72 4. £37.50 plus £2.50 p&p (NB This larger work does not attract the standard p&p of £1.50).

📖 **Introduction to Prisons and Imprisonment** Nick Flynn. With a Foreword by Lord Hurd of Westwell CH CBE PC. An ideal introduction for people needing a basic but broad overview of the system. Under the auspices of the Prison Reform Trust. ISBN 1 872 870 37 6. £12

📖 **Punishments of Former Days** Ernest W Pettifer The history of punishment in Britain from early times until the outbreak of World War II. A good read *The Magistrate.* ISBN 1 872 870 05 8. £9.50

📖 **Children Who Kill** Paul Cavadino (Ed.) With contributions by **Gitta Sereny** and others. From the tragic Mary Bell and Jamie Bulger cases to comparable events world-wide. Highly recommended *The Law.* A rich source of information *BJSW.* (1996) ISBN 1 872 870 29 5. £16

📖 **Hanging in the Balance** Brian Block and John Hostettler A history of the abolition of capital punishment in Britain. **Foreword: Lord Callaghan** (who was home secretary at the time). A masterwork *Justice of the Peace.* (1997) ISBN 1 872 870 47 3. £18

📖 **Introduction to Road Traffic Offences** Winston Gordon, Philip Cuddy. (see also *The Sentence of the Court* Series). A complete overview of this everyday topic. Includes lists of endorsement codes and penalty points, and solid basic information on such topics as dangerous and careless driving, drink driving, disqualification and document offences. Excellent value. (1998) ISBN 1 872 870 51 1. £12

📖 **Juvenile Delinquents and Young People in Danger** Willie McCarney (Ed.). An international survey of the way juvenile offenders are treated/dealt with. In association with the International Association of Juvenile and Family Court Magistrates. (1996) ISBN 1 872 870 39 2

📖 **Deaths of Offenders: The Hidden Side of Justice** Alison Liebling (Ed). In association with the Institute for the Study and Treatment of Delinquency (ISTD). A survey of deaths in police, prison and special hospital custody, including on remand and in police cells. (1998) ISBN 1 872 870 61 9. £16

Also from Waterside Press

Also from Waterside Press

Introduction to Criminology A Basic Guide

Russell Pond A lay person's guide written with people working in the criminal justice arena in mind. The basic ideas of criminology and their sources.
1998 ISBN 1 872 870 42 2. £12

Criminal Classes Offenders at School

Angela Devlin
If you are in any doubt about the links between poor education, crime and recidivism, read it: Marcel Berlins *The Guardian*.
First reprint, 1997 ISBN 1 872 870 30. £16

Drugs, Trafficking and Criminal Policy

Penny Green
A comprehensive account of the current state of play including the argument that concentrating on 'low-level' players acts as a diversion from more important issues.
1998 ISBN 1 872 870 33 3. £18

Drinking and Driving

Jonathan Black
Strongly recommended *Justice of the Peace* 1993 ISBN 1 872 870 12 0. £14

Hanging in the Balance

Brian Block and John Hostettler A history of the abolition of capital punishment in Britain. **Foreword: Lord Callaghan.** A masterwork *Justice of the Peace*.
1997 ISBN 1 872 870 47 3. £18

Domestic Violence

Chris Bazell and Bryan Gibson A key work which surveys the nature and extent of domestic violence and deals with the main legal remedies, including non-molestation, occupation of the family home and the interface with the Protection From Harassment Act 1997.
1998 ISBN 1 872 870 60 0. £18

Conflict Resolution A Foundation Guide

Susan Stewart
Of interest to people who deal with disputes, including through mediation and alternative dispute resolution procedures.
1998 ISBN 1 872 870 65 1. £12